The Best Love, The Best Sex

Creating Sensuous, Soulful, Supersatisfying Relationships

- We need to change our sexual attitudes if we expect to change our sexual behavior.

- Intercourse should be redesigned so that it becomes a mutually satisfying sexual expression.

- Don't place your partner's desire ahead of your own—sex is supposed to be an equal-opportunity experience.

- Learn to show and tell your partner your sexual needs and wants.

- No one is responsible for your sexual satisfaction but you— learn to take charge of your own orgasm.

"These are the beliefs I live by, the commonsense sexual inspiration you'll find inside this book. And I promise you, I won't ask you anything about your sex life until I share my own mistakes and triumphs. I'll give you the courage to be honest with yourself and your partner. You have the right to become sexually proud and confident. And you deserve *The Best Love, The Best Sex*."

—Suzi Landolphi

D0650553

Most Perigee Books are available at special quantity discounts for bulk purchases for sales promotions, premiums, fund-raising or educational use. Special books, or book excerpts, can also be created to fit specific needs.

For details, write: Special Markets, The Berkley Publishing Group, 200 Madison Avenue, New York, New York 10016.

The Best Love, The Best Sex

CREATING SENSUOUS, SOULFUL, SUPERSATISFYING RELATIONSHIPS

Suzi Landolphi

INDIANAPOLIS MARION CO. PUBLIC LIBRARY

A Perigee Book

A Perigee Book
Published by The Berkley Publishing Group
200 Madison Avenue
New York, NY 10016

Copyright © 1996 by Suzi Landolphi
Book design by Carol Malcolm Russo/Signet M Design, Inc.
Cover design by Joe Lanni
Cover photograph of author © by Pam Springsteen

All rights reserved. This book, or parts thereof, may not be reproduced in
any form without permission.

First G. P. Putnam's Sons edition: October 1996
First Perigee edition: October 1997
Perigee ISBN: 0-399-52341-3

Published simultaneously in Canada.

The Putnam Berkley World Wide Web site address is
http://www.berkley.com

The Library of Congress has catalogued the G. P. Putnam's Sons edition as
follows:

Landolphi, Suzi.
The best love, the best sex: creating sensuous, soulful,
supersatisfying relationships / by Suzi Landolphi
p.   cm.
ISBN 0-399-14163-4
1. Sex.   2. Pleasure.   3. Love.   4. Man-woman relationships.   I. Title.
HQ21.L233   1996
306.7—dc20   96-16210 CIP

PRINTED IN THE UNITED STATES OF AMERICA
10   9   8   7   6   5   4   3   2   1

The words and thoughts expressed in this book are
dedicated to my husband, David:
For giving my daughter the love she needs and deserves,
For nurturing all who enter our home,
For living the best love and the best sex.
Know that you are and forever appreciated and cherished
with all my love and respect.

I-MCPL

Thank-yous Are So Important

Writing this book was like a great sexual experience because the little bit I did alone was very satisfying and with the rest of the book, I had a lot of wonderful help, nurturing, and fun with a partner, Linda Tomchin. We laughed a lot and had many heartfelt, intense conversations about what we hoped others would get from our work and experiences. She was honest with me, and I trusted her input. She cared about the message as much as the messenger. She shared her stories and sorted through mine, making sure they were accessible and helpful. She is one of my inspirations and I never want to write another book without her gentle, loving wisdom to guide me. THANK YOU, LCT—THE GODDESS.

As I run to and fro through this world, talking up a sexual storm, I am always eternally grateful for Tina Mabry's calm voice. If I am the hurricane—she is the eye! THANK YOU, TINA. You have triumphed this year, and now it's time for you to take your turn.

I am blessed with so many people who have encouraged my journey and my work:

Renee and David Sams: You created the BEST LOVE infomercial, never asking me to dilute or change my message or my passion.

Jennifer Rogers: You had the vision and tenacity to put my message on-line on the WWW.

Christopher DeLouise: You are paying your price without complaints or excuses and helping so many who are lost find a better way.

Suzanne Bober, editor: You will lead your generation into the new millennium with better-written and -edited words. You have made my voice stronger and my ideas clearer.

Kyrsha, my daughter: You had to live through my darkest hours and feel the pain of my mistakes. Now, we can both enjoy the benefits and heal from our achievements. Thank you for forgiving me and staying close so that your children can reap the harvest of sexual self-worth and confidence—assuring that we, as a community, will never go back into our fear.

And

my husband, David Pritchard: You made the idea of *The Best Love, The Best Sex* a reality. The journey to you seemed very difficult at times, yet now I am hardly con-

scious of its memory. I guess it's like giving birth: the reward is far greater than the work—worth every pain. I am
so grateful for your love and friendship and for our sexual
life. If many look to me for sexual guidance, I learn from
you. You are a true partner, and I thank you for all your
encouragement and inspiration. You are THE BEST
LOVE and THE BEST SEX.

Contents

Foreword: A Letter to My Readers

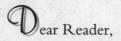

Dear Reader,

I was meeting with some people after one of my BEST LOVE, BEST SEX presentations, and a woman about my age asked a question that no one had ever asked me before; "How did you get to where you are—I mean, emotionally, how did you get to be so sexually proud and confident?" I hadn't even thought about it. I was so busy trying to fix and change my own sexual attitudes that I never stopped to look at the journey I took to get there. I couldn't reflect on my sexual past until I was firmly in the present.

I'm in a much better place than I've ever been, and it's getting better all the time. Actually, I'm in the BEST LOVE and having the BEST SEX. I had to go through a few—no, many—trials and tribulations along the road to finding my self-worth and becoming a real partner in a relationship. It wasn't bad luck; it was wrong choices and a gross lack of self-esteem. I made some mistakes more than

once, more than twice, sometimes more than I care to remember—but I did, eventually, achieve my goal, to become sexually proud and confident.

I'm going to share my mistakes, failures, triumphs,
and tools in the hope of inspiring you to start your own
sexual evolution. I will go first, telling my story, so that
you can feel safer reshaping and redesigning your sexual
attitudes and behavior. It's all about moving past shame and
judgment. Every day we carry on our backs heavy imag-
inary sacks filled with shame, guilt, embarrassment, mis-
information, and fear about our sexuality. We bring these
"sacks" into every relationship with family, friends, and
lovers; and their negativity overpowers any hope for honest and positive sexual exchange. It's time to empty out
our sacks and take charge of our sexual self-worth.

Every evolutionary gain starts with an individual desire for a higher consciousness and a better quality of life.
The human spirit will always seek greater understanding
and the tools to build that which encourages love and life.
We cannot survive without human love, affection, and
connection. We should not have to live in darkness or fear
about our own sexuality. It is our human and spiritual right
to be fully aware and in charge of our sexual desires and
actions.

For me, it was a need for total personal honesty and
detailed sexual information that helped me start my journey. You can do the same. Everyone can become sexually proud and confident and create the best love and the
best sex. It's not just for those with academic credentials

or lots of worldly experience. Regardless of where you are now or where you come from, you can make your sexuality one of the most positive, fulfilling, and fun parts of your life. It's your right.

Without sexual self-worth, we can stumble and fall into the deepest and most vicious despair. It can destroy other areas of our life and weaken every relationship we try to build. The lack of sexual self-esteem and knowledge has been our greatest failure as a society and I, for one, feel that I cannot let it continue. If we can design new cars every year to improve travel comfort and safety for ourselves and those we love, we can do no less for our sex lives. Just think about it: this book is a lot cheaper and easier to maintain than a new car! AND it can bring you to newer and much better places—places that can lift your spirit and bring you closer to those you love. Enjoy the journey, keep your eyes open; and tell everyone you meet the sexual truth. Send me a postcard telling where you ended up and about all the fun you're having.

You deserve no less,

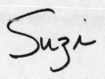

The
Best Love,
The
Best Sex

CHAPTER ONE

A Healthy Sex Life Begins with Exploring the Attitudes Formed in Our Youth

To do it, or not to do it? I'm confused, are you?

WE ARE SEXUAL FROM BIRTH TO DEATH

YOU MAY BE WONDERING why and how I got started on this quest for the best love and the best sex. Like most discoveries, it started with my own inability to create a satisfying partnership and sex life. Even though I learned some valuable lessons in my teen years, I was by no means sexually confident. As an adult, I fell in and out of relationships and sexual experiences, and wondered what was wrong with me. But I couldn't change my behavior until I changed my attitudes about myself and my

sexuality. In fact, it was impossible to improve my relationships and sex life until I uncovered the misconceptions
and fears that were a part of my upbringing. In order to
discard those sexual ideas and behaviors that are blocking
your understanding and happiness, you must be willing to
evaluate your old beliefs and actions taught by parents,
teachers, religious instructors, and peers. By telling you my
story, my aim is to encourage you to examine yours.
When you know how and why your sexual attitudes came
to be, it will be much easier for you to change unwanted
behavior and make smart choices. Keep your heart and
mind open, and don't be afraid to try a new idea!

Let's begin with the concept that we are sexual beings
from birth until death. This is pretty obvious to those of
us who have children. When we change their diapers, the
first thing babies do is to grab their genitals and put their
feet in their ears to get a really good grip (some of us wish
we could still do that!). However, what do we say to the
baby? "No, no, mustn't touch. Dirty, dirty!" And what is
the baby thinking? *Gee, Mom and Dad, if you did this more
often, you'd be less stressed!* The baby is right. This comfort
and fascination with our genitals starts even earlier. Baby
boys have erections while still in their mother's womb, and
baby girls discover their genitals at this time, too.

Some of our earliest memories of sexuality and sexual
differences are accompanied by negativity rather than
truthful and specific explanations. We feel the comfort of
our own genitals along with terrible confusion. We are
told not to touch the parts that make us feel good. Why?
"Because I said so!" is the response most often heard. We
continue to explore these sensations in secret because we
have a terrible fear of getting caught or being punished.

As boys and girls, we play games like *"Doctor"* in order to show and tell. When adults aren't around, we continue our explorations with our best friends, usually those of the same sex. After all, boys are *icky,* and girls are *a pain,* so who better to play with than your best friend? This natural rubbing and touching seems okay to us until we get teased about liking the same sex, and then we begin to have more shame and guilt rather than sexual self-esteem.

As our sexual energy continues to develop, society tries even harder to control our sexual expressions. We get reprimanded by Mom and Dad, other family members, friends, school, church, TV, and anyone who believes that they have the right to be the sex police. No real information is given, just a lot of contradictory *don'ts.* The only *do*'s we get are the ones used to sell us something. Advertisers have no qualms about using sex to sell their products.

On top of our growing confusion, we are bombarded with myths of gender difference. We are pulled apart as boys and girls, taught to believe that we are sexual adversaries, and then we are pushed together again in adulthood. We are forced to start our sex lives as sexually embarrassed illiterates. The natural childhood curiosity and sexual pride that we once had is quickly replaced by misconceptions and shame.

We enter puberty with fear and confusion, and the only thing we're taught is how the sperm meets the egg. Erections, wet dreams, and desire in our jeans are never discussed. There is little information about our emerging sexuality. For girls, periods come unannounced, and along with our embarrassment or disgust, we become the butt of many jokes. No one knows how to give us any real information or comfort. For boys, it's just as frustrating. Erections come and go with no warning or control, and boys are left to feel vulnerable in the locker room, or the YMCA pool, or standing at the blackboard. Wet dreams turn into nightmares when no one has explained that they are a natural sexual expression for boys, and that girls have them too.

Remember the sex talk that most of us didn't get? We don't want sex education in our schools, but it's rarely taught at home. A lack of correct information only encourages more sexual activity in teenagers. What if driver's ed were taught like sex ed? *Okay, kids, here's the key—now find the hole in the car it belongs to. Now stick it in the hole, turn on your engine, and step on the gas. Make sure you stay on the road. If you go too fast, slam on the brakes, and try to stop safely.* Good Luck!

Sex is the only subject about which we believe that the less we know, the better off we are. We certainly rush to learn about other important aspects of life and are willing to share our knowledge and experience about them, but not sexuality. It's no wonder that we turn any "dirty" book, magazine, or videotape into our source of visuals. For many, this material is our first actual look at sex, and it depicts intercourse as something devoid of emotional or spiritual connection. Never mind that the pictures are enhanced and edited, and the people are just pretending. We are set up to have unreal expectations.

A LACK OF SEXUAL INFORMATION DOESN'T DETER SEXUAL ACTIVITY IN TEENS

MY HIGH-SCHOOL years greatly influenced my sexuality as an adult. When I was a teenager, a major event happened that helped me begin my journey toward sexual self-confidence. My sister got pregnant at sixteen. What a mess and heartache for all of us. I loved my sister, and I knew that she was in a desperate situation. My mother was her usual loving and supportive self; she was determined not to let this pull our already struggling family apart. My mom's boyfriend, who was, to me, my real dad (they eventually married), helped us cope with this difficult dilemma.

Ultimately, my sister had an abortion. Unfortunately, in those days abortion was not legal, except under certain circumstances, and this was not one of them. My sister and her boyfriend had intercourse because they thought they were in love, and that's what lovers do. My mother took my sister to a hellhole of an apartment in an area of Boston that should have been leveled. After some guy, not a doctor, gave my sister a drug to induce abortion, my mother was left to dispose of the fetus. It was horrible.

This family nightmare affected all of us. No one was to blame. It was what so many young men and women, and families, went through in secret. Sex out of wedlock was never discussed in those days, let alone unintended pregnancy, which was shameful and potentially ruinous for the entire family. This type of tragedy was a result of society's taboos about sex. We are taught to have such shame and guilt about our sexuality, yet we use sex as a symbol for all that is successful and powerful. It's such a contradiction, and our young people suffer for it.

So, what is a person to do when faced with such conflicting messages? Do it! Don't do it! Do it! Don't!

GIRLS ARE TAUGHT THAT THEIR SEXUAL FEELINGS CAN HURT THEM

I KNOW MY sister went through hell as a young girl. She was overweight most of her life. I was present when my biological dad called her "fat" whenever we went shopping for school clothes. Even as a kid, I knew she felt ashamed about her looks. And there I was, the cute little dancer, praised and coddled, while she flipped hamburgers at the dance studio snack bar. In other words, I was the darling; she was the fat girl.

Then one day, one of the most popular guys at our high school started to pay attention to her. He teased her with an arrogant attitude, and she threw it right back at him. No one could give "shit" like my sister. She could cut anyone down to size, quicker than slicing a tomato, and then grind him up into her next cheeseburger. No one ever stood up to this big shot, especially a chubby snack bar girl. As his attention grew into respect, and the respect grew into love, he was hooked. Here was a girl, strong and self-confident, who wasn't impressed by his looks and talent. She was different from all the others, and he had to have her. Unfortunately, like so many of our personal strengths, my sister's came from deep hurt and pain, and was mostly a defense mechanism—a way to keep her lack of self-worth from showing; a way to fend off any more emotional attacks; a way to keep people away, so they couldn't get close enough to hurt her.

As he pursued her, attracted to her ballsy *I don't care who you are* attitude, she began to let down her defenses, and, eventually, the hurt little girl, with no real self-confidence, exposed herself. She so hoped this boy-man would understand her, and still like her—the real her—the one who desperately needed to be loved and validated.

She let him have intercourse with her to prove how much she loved and needed him, and, of course, the worst happened. As she replaced her so-called tough and confident self with submission and fear of losing his attention, he lost interest and left. Just more proof that no one could love *the real her*. He went off and scored again, and she was left pregnant, heartbroken, and with little self-respect.

There is a happy ending to this story. Today, my sister is the proud mother of two sons, and the grandmother of a beautiful baby grandson. She will always be one of my heroes.

Like every bad experience, my sister's struggle was an opportunity for growth and learning. For me, it led to a major moment of discovery about sex and self-worth. Sexual intercourse had brought so much pain to so many, and yet it was supposed to be an expression of love that brings two people closer together and creates a bond and commitment. I hadn't had intercourse yet and had only learned about it through the experiences of others, or TV, movies, and books.

From my fourteen-year-old vantage point, this one incident did a lot of damage. It had nothing to do with being a virgin. I didn't think any less of my sister because she expressed her love and devotion through sexual intercourse. To me, it was more about being rejected. I saw my sister in agony and pain, feeling so abandoned, when her boyfriend took the coward's way out and bolted. She was further than ever from realizing her own self-worth. My mom was truly shaken by this emotional explosion in our family and worried about my sister for many years to come. My introduction to sexual intercourse was like being introduced to someone who slaps your face instead of shaking your hand. The aftermath of having intercourse was so much more than a wet spot on the backseat of the car.

So I decided I wasn't going to do it. If I ever got pregnant, it would kill Mom and Dad. And then, the guy would leave me. In my mind, this intercourse thing was definitely not worth it. I didn't want to do it.

You CAN CONTROL YOUR OWN ORGASM

TWO YEARS HAVE passed, and Gary* and I are parked behind the Jewish cemetery. I hear crickets and catch glimpses of light from other cars searching for their own parking spots. I'm so sweaty and so excited. I feel like I'm going to explode. I've been with Gary for two years, but

---

*Not his real name. Names and identifying characteristics of certain individuals mentioned throughout the book have been changed to protect their privacy.

our relationship has progressed slowly, very slowly. He is even more shy than I am when it comes to making out.

We must have spent a whole year just kissing every which way we could, trading spit and tongues, until one of us had to admit defeat and go home. It was a perfect relationship until our desire to do more started to creep up on us. I was more adventurous than Gary and kept inching my way onto his body, searching for a way to rub my crotch on anything I could find. Of course, we didn't talk. We did this like two mimes with our eyes closed, trying to read each other's body language, while our lips were superglued together. At the time, I knew: 1. I was very sexually aroused and wanted to discover my own sexual satisfaction. I don't think I used the word *orgasm* then, but I knew I wanted to reach a new sexual level. 2. I didn't want to have intercourse. I wasn't physically or emotionally ready for intercourse. I made a promise to myself after my sister's experience, yet I wanted to be sexual.

There I was in the front seat of a Valiant, with my crotch on fire, and no real instructions on what to do, other than putting his penis in my vagina.

Everyone on TV and in the movies had intercourse, or else they just stopped and went home frustrated. Neither was an option for me. I wanted more. Using our hands for arousal and exploring was fine, but somewhere I picked up the idea that mutual masturbation was perverted, and certainly not *real sex*. None of my friends ever said: "Oh, we just rubbed each other down there with our hands until we both exploded." Instead my girlfriends' stories all sounded the same: *We French-kissed. He went under my blouse and rubbed my breasts and undid my bra. He undid my pants, and I helped him pull them down. He undid his pants,*

but I never really saw IT. He lay on top and put it in. He moved;
he came; he got off.

Determined to get some sexual relief, I took the lead
and mounted this skinny, long-legged young man and
pressed my pelvis into his, feeling for anything I could find.
I would have settled for a *chapstick* tube in his pants pocket.
To my surprise and delight, he had something much more
effective: his erection. An erect penis is such a great design, especially when constricted under chinos and briefs
(or when the owner arranges it in a vertical direction for
his own comfort). It didn't matter to me how it got there;
it mattered that it was there, and I had something perfect
to rub against. Even though we were fully clothed, there
was enough sensation to take me higher and closer to sexual spontaneous combustion.

I felt in control because I was on top. It's not that I
demanded the control; it's simply that Gary didn't seem
to mind. He went along with the ride, and from what I
could tell, he physically liked it. He moaned a little, he
pressed back, but he never grabbed my butt to add more
leverage. I'm glad he didn't because it left me free to move
and explore. As I got more excited and pressed harder and
faster, he went deeper into his own pleasure.

The first couple of times we got close to orgasm, we
stopped. No, I stopped. I remember thinking, *Do I want*
to jump off this cliff? Do I want to go to this new and exciting
place? I felt a little fear, a little embarrassment, and a little
reluctance to reach the prize and end an era of sexual exploration. It was so much fun getting there; I only hoped
the actual orgasm was as thrilling.

We kept rubbing harder. I discovered that I had to
align just the right spot on my crotch with his erect penis.

If I was too far to the left or right, I didn't get enough stimulation. Soon, we became experts and lined up the right spots with every slide and rub. Once in a while I would sneak a peak at the expression on his face. Even with his eyes closed, I could see that going unconscious look, and the sexual pleasure smile pulling at the corners of his mouth. It was working for both of us. I noticed that as I got more excited, so did he. It was like laughing together—one person starts to chuckle, and without any coaching, that person's laughter ignites the other's, and this "laughing gas" passes back and forth until you're both wiping tears from your eyes. It was just like that. As we moved together, our sexual ecstasy was catching—we were giving each other permission with our rising heartbeats, pelvic presses, and swollen genitals.

When we finally reached orgasm, I will never forget the quake that went through my body—the electrical charge that pulsated in my pelvis, the pounding of my heart, and the almost unconscious feeling in my head. He rattled, too. Then we both relaxed in our sweat-drenched oxford shirts and chinos. My crotch was still sensitive, but not screaming at me to keep pushing, as it was during those last few minutes. I smiled because I couldn't help myself. It must be part of the orgasm. Involuntary genital spasms and then an involuntary smile.

I slowly peeled myself off Gary, and looked at his face for some kind of reaction. His eyes were half closed, and he had the same stupid grin on his face. We straightened ourselves out, and as he tucked his shirt back into his pants, I noticed a wet spot right next to his zipper. Yes, he was as wet as I was. He had ejaculated, and so had I. We felt great! Pleased with ourselves for figuring out a way to have an orgasm without intercourse. And I was especially proud because I had been the sexually assertive one. By changing prescribed roles, we made the situation fit us as individuals. He didn't have to be the aggressor, and I didn't have to be the passive one.

For the next three years, Gary and I had lots of orgasms, and I always wondered if his mom noticed those wet spots on his chinos.

Good SEX IS A STEP-BY-STEP PROCESS

MY EXPERIENCE WITH Gary taught me that *sex was more than intercourse.* As a young adult, I could be sexual and not have to do something that I wasn't ready for. I learned that sex is a step-by-step process, and we needed time before connecting our genitals. First, we had to build an emotional connection. Then we had to understand our individual sexual desires. Mine pushed me to touch more skin and rub a little harder. I became aware of how my sexual energy hung around me everywhere, like a pestering kid sister wanting more attention than I wanted to give. I learned about creative problem solving. It was possible to find a satisfying alternative to a very strong and demanding need. Gary and I discovered a way to bring both of us to orgasm without the worry of getting pregnant.

Our sex life was satisfying; we were getting more out of it than most of our friends. Yet, by society's standards, we were not doing *the real thing.* And even though Gary humped, banged, and grunted on me, I wasn't going home feeling like I was broken because I didn't have an orgasm during intercourse (like most of my girlfriends). And I didn't feel used. My partner wasn't getting a locker room ego boost describing my most intimate parts as if they were new chrome bumpers for his car.

Why didn't anyone ever tell us we could do it like this? Why were all the adults still bitching and complaining about teens getting pregnant, when all they had to do was tell us how to be sexual in a way that was great for having orgasms and didn't put anyone at risk? Was it because they didn't know? Or was intercourse considered the only real sex? Or if the woman takes control, is on top, was she too dominating? All these thoughts went through my mind.

As I think back to my teenage sexual encounters, I realize how much they still influence me as an adult. All that I discovered with Gary is still relevant to me now. I use the same step-by-step process to intercourse. Gary's satisfaction was not more important than mine; we were equal participants adding activities to our sexual repertoire through mutual agreement. We stumbled on good ideas for building a successful partnership as teens that still apply to my more sophisticated adult sex life. Of course, the reverse can be true. If mutual satisfaction, or sharing the sexual control, isn't part of our first sexual experiences, it can be difficult to change as adults. As I analyze my sexual escapades with Gary, I realize how confident I felt during our explorations. I can honestly say I haven't always felt that way during my adult sexual relationships.

MOST OF US HAVE THE WRONG SEXUAL INFORMATION

FOR MOST OF our teen years, we stumble and struggle and never experience any positive sexual success. Most
of us continue this struggle all through our adult lives. Instead of learning the correct information, we try to figure
out this sex thing ourselves as society continues to push
these contradictory messages down our throats:

• **Sex equals intercourse.** This one sex act is
supposed to be the only real sex. Nothing could
be further from the sexual truth. Putting so much
emphasis on this one sexual expression unfairly
limits our chances of creating a broader and more
individualistic definition of mutually satisfying sexuality.

• **Wait until marriage before having sex.** It's
an idealistic message but not very realistic. What
it really means is wait to have intercourse. It reinforces the belief that intercourse is the only way to
have sex and invalidates other ways to sexually express ourselves.

• **Sex will reward you with power, money,
and acceptance.** This message is hammered into
our consciousness through television, movies, and
advertisements. It makes our sexuality a commod-

ity that can be bartered. We are led to believe that we can separate our sexuality from our emotional and spiritual being. Ultimately, when we meet that special partner and try to combine sex and love, we find we are too scared to be truly vulnerable and intimate.

• **Sex is easy to do.** Why then are so many of us unhappy and unsatisfied with our sex lives? Great sex is not that easy to achieve, certainly not as easy as it looks in movies or on television. However, with the correct information and guidance, *everyone* is capable of being a great sexual partner.

• **Sex will give you horrible diseases, or even worse, kill you.** Fear will never stop people from being sexual. But we must change the way we use sexuality and the conditions under which we engage in its expression. Some sexual expressions put us more at risk, physically and emotionally, when done out of desperation or with little or no information.

• **Sex is love. Love is sex.** Neither is correct by itself. Love can be expressed through sex, but sex alone doesn't express love. Sex is most satisfying when expressed with love.

• **Sex with yourself is bad and perverted. Sex with a stranger is okay.** Where did we get this backwards reasoning? By making masturbation a shameful act, or only for undesirables who can't

get a partner, we have subliminally established the
idea that having sex with a stranger is better. Sex
with yourself is an expression of self-love and promotes genital health and a stronger immune system.

• **Sex ends when you get married because
variety is the spice of life.** My experience has
been just the opposite. I have faked sexual pleasure more often with someone I didn't know well
enough. The best sex will always come with real
honesty and real emotional and physical safety.
That means no embarrassment or judgment, and
real concern for the sexual, physical, emotional,
and spiritual well-being of both partners. A variety of sexual expressions with a loving and re-
spectful partner is the spice of my sex life.

• **Only those people who look sexy are sexy.**
The media started this ugly rumor by using sex, sex
appeal, and sexiness to sell us the illusion of sexual
power and desire. Sexy is a state of mind. How you
think about who you are as a sexual person is an
attitude that is based on positive sexual self-worth
and not a certain look, fashion trend, or an actor's
performance. Sexy is what we do with our sexuality, not what we look like.

All these contradictory messages set us up to be sexual failures, and the biggest confusion surrounds intercourse. It would be healthier to teach young people a
step-by-step approach to intercourse that involves:

1. having orgasms together before having intercourse,
2. allowing women to take charge of their sex life
and orgasms, and
3. encouraging each partner to find his and her
own pleasure spot so each has equal satisfaction.

BUILD YOUR SEX LIFE
ONE PLEASURE AT A TIME

IN A STEP-BY-STEP approach to sex, common sense
tells us to take it slowly and build one pleasure-filled experience upon the next. Yet how many times have we
fooled around during a new sexual encounter and found
ourselves going from a few passionate kisses to full-fledged
intercourse? Wait! How did we get there so fast?

We go into the acting like we like it mode and think
to ourselves, *I'll get the hang of this sooner or later*, or *I'm sure
I'll learn to like it eventually*, or *I'll tell him what I really like
next time*. What we're really thinking is, *I don't want to hurt
his feelings*, or *I'm too embarrassed*, or *I don't know her well
enough to "show and tell" this early in the relationship*.

Where did we get this backwards logic? It plainly
shows a lack of sexual common sense. Is it from all those
movies that show people having intercourse within five
minutes of meeting each other? Wait a second! In a movie,
the director has only three minutes for the sex scene, so
several sex steps are omitted, edited, and left on the cutting-
room floor. It's called dramatic license. In real life, the one
you and I take part in, it doesn't work that way. We don't

have a director standing at the edge of the bed, guiding every move, touch, and moan. We have to direct the scene ourselves, and editing is definitely not a part of it.

Like every other complex and emotionally charged activity between two people, great sex needs a step-by-step pleasure foundation. In other words, sex is a physical, emotional, and spiritual transaction that gets its momentum from building upon successive pleasurable acts. The honesty and care of the first touch or kiss sets the groundwork for the next pleasure steps. Each pleasure step is based upon the one before it and helps to build a mutually satisfying sexual pathway to the next pleasure level.

Think of this sexual-pleasure-step principle as if you were an architect, engineer, builder, or seamstress crafting your creation. Start at ground level, taking your next step when the first steps have been completed with utmost care and satisfaction. Don't move to step two until you are completely comfortable with step one. In fact, stay there awhile enjoying the newness and excitement of it all. If you have been honest with each other, you can enjoy the next level of sexual pleasure.

Take one sexual step at a time. Build your sexual pleasure foundation. Any structure, any relationship, is only as strong as its foundation.

SEX DOES NOT EQUAL INTERCOURSE

I DID NOT REALIZE it then, but Gary and I had turned our backs on the norm—the way sex between a man and a woman is often portrayed and achieved. We didn't follow the gender rules; we didn't use intercourse as THE way to be sexual. The real change in us was in our attitudes. It seemed so simple. A commonsense approach to entering the world of partner sex. Sex now included any and all ways to have an orgasm. The man didn't have to always take charge, and the woman didn't have to passively lie on her back. I didn't think of myself as "the erection releaser," so I didn't act like one.

I was lucky enough to figure this out early in life. By using the word *sex* when we really mean *vaginal intercourse,* we put ourselves in a very difficult sexual position. We have all been brainwashed into believing this erroneous idea—one that has dominated our sexual choices and patterns for generations. And we wonder why each year more teens are getting pregnant, and why so many adults are still dissatisfied with their sex lives.

The belief that sex equals intercourse is a remnant from the past. It's old news that dates back to a time when pestilence, plague, and war destroyed nations. Intercourse was necessary to produce children and carry on civilization. Therefore, intercourse was the only necessary and important sexual act. Let's hope that these days we're more interested in birth control than repopulating a civilization.

Furthermore, in the old days, sex was intended to satisfy the man. Who cared if it didn't work so well for the woman? After all, women have the babies; that's satisfaction enough for them.

So, for eons, our picture of sex has been man and woman having intercourse. Anything else is called foreplay—the play before the main event or real sex. How fair is this? The idea that intercourse equals sex doesn't bring into consideration a woman's sexual needs or satisfaction.

In fact, most sex positions pictured in "how-to" manuals don't bring a majority of women to orgasm.

"Did you do *it*?" "Did you have *sex* yet?" "Are you still a *virgin*?" "Did you *sleep with* her yet?" "Did you get *it* on?"

It is intercourse; *sex* is intercourse. *Virgin* means not having intercourse. Of course, you can do everything else with everyone listed in the Yellow Pages and still call yourself a "virgin." *Sleep with* is another expression for intercourse. Why is it so difficult to use the actual word for this sexual act? Is it too explicit? Too EXPLICIT? How in the world are you going to talk about something as explicit as intercourse without using the word *intercourse*? Not to mention that we completely negate all other sexual expressions and make them unimportant or not worthy of being called *real sex*.

What's the solution? It's time to say what we mean. It's time for all of us to change our way of sexually communicating and say the words that describe the deed. If we were playing *Jeopardy,* and "Sex" was a category, "Intercourse" would be one of the answers.

Let's not continue to equate intercourse with the only real sex act. Instead, let's free ourselves and the generations to come, and have lots of great sexual acts from which to choose—ones that fit our emotional, physical, and spiritual maturity. Ones that fit our relationships. Ones that fit our levels of commitment. Ones that don't put us at risk. Ones that mutually satisfy both partners. Now, that is real sex.

WOMEN ARE SEXUAL, NOT SEX OBJECTS

As A TEENAGER I discovered I liked feeling sexually confident and not having to wait for Gary to make all the sexual advances and decisions. I liked feeling good about what we were doing and how well we did it. I was learning to be a sexual individual and equal partner. Many of my girlfriends waited to be called for their sex time—after the hockey game, or time with *his* friends. They believed that being desired, or being used, was the best they could hope for.

Besides, many of them had their first intercourse experience with boys they couldn't even talk to or count on as friends. They went out with boys who constantly brushed them aside, or only saw them on Saturday nights for a movie and intercourse. Others believed they were in love, yet, there were constant arguments and breakups. Well, that happens to most young lovers, but when things got bad with their boyfriends, whom did they turn to for solace? Their "boy" friends! You know, those boys who we could always talk to about anything and everything, even sex. These boys treated us better than our so-called boyfriends. They were the ones with whom we felt so safe and comfortable. I was the weirdo who thought it strange to have an intercourse experience with someone who wasn't really a friend. Why don't we have intercourse with *these* boys?!

Why was it so perverted to have a sexual experience with a friend? I didn't talk about this idea anymore, but I thought about it a great deal. It made more sense than going out with some Dick (pardon the pun) and having intercourse with a total stranger. But my idea defied all those romantic notions that girls kept seeing in movies or reading in romance novels. My sister would have been better off if her first lover also had been her friend. All women would be better off if their lovers were also their friends.

As I learned that my sexual satisfaction was as important as Gary's, it was okay to go after it. I was having orgasms and not worrying about getting pregnant! It was the same for Gary—a win-win situation for both of us. I learned one more important piece of information from all that pelvic grinding and groping. I had orgasms from rubbing a certain area that was located on the outside of my vagina. Would it be the same when a penis was in my vagina? Maybe. I wasn't sure. And I wasn't in such a hurry to find out.

SEXUAL SELF-ESTEEM BUILDS PERSONAL SELF-WORTH

MY SEXUAL SELF-CONFIDENCE flowed into other areas of my life. It was a time that I felt good about me and in control of my life. I knew my mom would be proud of me—proud that I had figured out how to be sexual and not put myself at risk for pregnancy. That boosted my self-confidence the most. Knowing that I could explore my sexuality, without hurting anyone or disappointing those who loved me, I felt more assured about my decisions. Later, when I found myself in painful adult sexual situations, I could think back to those moments, like the one with Gary, and tap into that sexual self-confidence once again. If I could make my way through all the pubescent confusion of a teenager, surely I could rise to the occasion as an adult. So many times we give up, or give in, during unhappy sexual situations. But I didn't as a teen, nor as an adult. I used the small but powerful seed of sexual self-confidence all through my adult years, especially when my self-worth had been battered or drained.

My mother was the person I had to thank. She was a big influence on my attitudes about being a woman and being sexual. I was always amazed at how easy it was to talk to my mother about sexuality, considering that her mother never talked to her about sex, or when she did, it was to shame her or make sure sex was viewed as a dirty part of life. I remember my mother telling me about times when she was a toddler, and my grandmother would wake her from a nap and smell her fingers to make sure she hadn't played with her genitals.

Mom wanted to help us kids have a better attitude about sexuality and have correct sexual information. She was the one who taught me about self-worth and love. She taught me to take care of myself and be more concerned about my own well-being than about someone else's orgasm. She had great words of wisdom and great expressions such as, *"Even though you helped to create an erection, you are not responsible for fixing it."* My mother had a wonderful sense of humor and never hesitated to use it. She spent many a night around the kitchen table, not only talking to me about sexuality and self-esteem, but she also stayed up late talking to my girlfriends, even Gary. She stressed the importance of friendship in love relationships, which was so apparent in her own healthy, loving relationship with my stepdad. Mom was definitely way ahead of her time, and now it's my turn to carry the torch for sexual empowerment and pass it on to my daughter's generation.

EVERYONE HAS THE RIGHT TO BECOME SEXUALLY PROUD AND CONFIDENT

I LEARNED THROUGH my sister's experience—it shaped my attitudes about sex and taught me the importance of empowering those we love with the right to be sexually proud and confident.

But how can we expect to become more mature in our sexual thoughts and behaviors when we hide our heads like ostriches whenever the subject of sex is raised? Sexual knowledge and education are the keys to healthy sexual self-esteem. Yet those of us who advocate extensive sex education run the risk of being labeled immoral, or enemies of the family, or perpetrators of the moral decline of our society.

Knowing the truth about sexuality has such power. And ignorance about something so powerful is much more dangerous than the knowledge of it. How can we keep sexuality apart from any other human feeling and need?

Only good can come from having more knowledge about sex.

How dare we call ourselves a caring and civilized society when we allow sexuality to be used as a political pawn? Or worse yet, how can we allow it to be the basis for most of our advertising revenue, while our religious leaders preach that we must be saved from this—the greatest evil! Shame on us for going through one more day, month, year, and, perhaps, century, avoiding one of the most important obligations to our children. Let's not send the next generation out into this world making the same mistakes we did, and still do, because of our fear of sexual knowledge.

My sexual self-esteem dominated other areas of my teenage life. As head of the cheerleading squad, I hated how girls' sports were not taken as seriously as the boys'. We never cheered at the girls' games. I once asked the cheerleading squad to root for the girls' basketball team, and I was met with looks the likes of which reminded me of deer frozen in headlights.

This sexual self-confidence had a major impact on all my attitudes. I was the first girl ever to run for student council in my school. It was scary, but I ran anyway. I was elected the first "girl" vice president. If I could take charge of my late-night parking sessions with Gary, I certainly could run a student council. For too long society said I couldn't, or shouldn't, be in charge of something, and I was breaking all the rules and stereotypes.

BOYS ARE TAUGHT THAT THEY ARE ENTITLED TO SEXUAL SATISFACTION

DURING MY SENIOR YEAR, Gary and I temporarily broke up, and I accepted a date with the captain of the football team. Alex was tall and handsome, yet I wasn't very attracted to him. He had an arrogant air about him, as if he were doing me a big favor asking me out. He had "entitlement" written all over him. I went out anyway, thinking we were going to a movie and maybe to Friendly's for ice cream. To my surprise, he drove straight to the local parking spot and proceeded to try to kiss me. I was furious. If I had wanted to make out with him, I would have told him so. Furthermore, I told him the date was over.

What a jerk! Alex was pissed, which made me even more angry. Who did he think he was? I know who *he* thought he was—the football hero entitled to every girl at school, and in control of when, where, and how he would have a sexual experience with any of them. Why would Suzi be different? He would be the one to get the head cheerleader to "give it up," or, at least, live up to the title of "head" cheerleader. He believed he had more of a right to my body, my sexuality, than I did. I was disgusted by his attitude more than his behavior. Too bad. This football player tried to do an end run and ran into a mean blocker.

As long as I knew the truth, what could Alex really do to me? But, on Monday, rumors swept through high school like a desert brushfire.

ALEX HAD SEX WITH SUZI LANDOLPHI.

I can't ever remember feeling so enraged, and so vic-
timized. Nothing had happened, except Alex's ego was
bruised. I confronted him at school, and called him every
name in the book, trying desperately to hang on to my
power. I felt like the little kid, and he was the big bully.
(You know the kind—he holds your ball over his head,
teasing you, as you grab desperately at air, trying to retrieve
it.) Alex laughed at me and walked away; we never talked
again. Fortunately, my self-esteem was intact. I had the
courage and tenacity to stand up for myself. I was not able
to get him to retract his lie, but I made him face me, and
feel my power.

Sexism is just another bad attitude

I WAS INFURIATED with Alex's sexist attitude and his
belief that he had a right to my body. I still have such a
difficult time with this kind of sexism. For me, it is perfectly obvious that one gender is not more powerful than
the other. Likewise, one gender is not more valuable than
the other. We are all of equal value! What else needs to
be said? Only those who believe in their own selfish gain,
power, and control would ever subscribe to anything other
than equality. Men and women are different, but difference doesn't denote less or more value. We are actually
more similar than different. Somehow, we seem to put
more emphasis on our differences than our similarities.

Sexism is an attitude, and attitudes are very changeable, but only if those with the sexist attitudes want to

change. Too many men with sexist attitudes have been in control of too much for too long. This imbalance doesn't hurt only women, it also hinders men in their quest for true personal power. Nothing is accomplished when one group puts down another to raise themselves up. True power is not about controlling other people. It's knowing that all people have an inherent right to control themselves and their own lives.

If we allow even one person to display sexist behavior because we fear him, then we become his accomplices. We may reroute our own thoughts, attitudes, and behaviors so that we don't have to confront "bullies." We may even start to believe their sexist attitudes, and put ourselves down in the process. You can't change another person's attitudes, but you don't have to put up with his behavior. And you certainly can let your own attitudes be known and heard loud and clear.

Behavior in the bedroom won't change until one or both partners gives up, or stops putting up with, sexist attitudes. Sexual satisfaction can only be experienced when each has mutual respect for the other.

$\mathcal{B}$UILDING MY SEX LIFE ON A FIRM FOUNDATION

MY SISTER, Gary, my mother, and the football team captain all played a part in forming my attitudes about sexuality and intercourse. These were the first bricks laid in a foundation that would eventually house my sexual self-worth.

- Sex is not just intercourse.
- Everyone has the right to be in charge of his or her own sexuality.
- If you're not friends, don't have intercourse.
- Successful sexuality is a step-by-step process.

CHAPTER TWO

Creating Relationships in Which Both Partners Are Equal

Sounds obvious to me!

SEXISM IS NOT SEXY IN ANY COUNTRY

IT WAS 1974. We had been in Australia for eighteen months, and it was time to go home. Mark, my husband at that time, was not as excited about returning home as I was. He had accomplished a lot, made friends, and furthered his career. I had accomplished a lot too, but my experience in Australia was very different.

I found Australia to be a country dictated by men to satisfy their needs and desires. Few of the women I knew had their driver's license or worked full-time. Most never went, or expected to go, to college. Man was king. He was in charge of family, lifestyle, and money. His wife was given a housekeeping allowance. After work, most husbands frequented a *No Women Allowed* pub to have a beer with their mates. I always thought it strange and disconcerting that Australian men used the word *mate* for a male friend, but not their real mates, as if it were sacrilegious for a wife to be a friend. By the way, the Aussie term for a woman is *Sheila,* as if one name for all women were sufficient. Actually, Australia was not an overtly hostile or abusive atmosphere for women, but men's needs certainly came first. In marriage, Australian women definitely were not considered equal partners.

While Mark seemed to thrive in this culture, I was suffocating. We started to disagree on fundamental beliefs about equality and marriage. I thought he truly believed in an equal partnership, but every time I tried to assert myself to fulfill my needs and goals, he put me down. Somehow, my wants and aspirations interfered with whatever he wanted. His career was always more important because he "made the money." His time at the pub was more important because he "worked hard all day." It was okay for him to be jealous if I talked to someone, but I was the "hysterical one" if I had similar feelings.

I thought, *Mark wasn't this way when I met him.* It must have been the influence of Australia's completely male-dominated culture. I was certain that we would do better when we returned to America. Back home, I planned to finish college, and Mark and I together would take care of our baby daughter, Kyrsha.

When it was time to leave, our Australian friends wanted to give us a going-away party. I was psyched for it. It felt as if I had been pregnant for years, and, now, six months after the birth of Kyrsha, I felt energized. I recently had my waist-length hair cut to a chic short style at the most trendy hair salon in Sydney. I was ready to bid farewell to Australia and begin my life anew back home.

WOMEN ARE TAUGHT THAT IT'S OKAY FOR SOMEONE ELSE TO TAKE CONTROL

MARK AND I shared a large, suburban brick house with John and Jane, two Aussies with whom we became friends the first week we arrived in Australia. They were married but had no children. Jane worked as a nurse's aid, and John did something in sales, but I wasn't sure what. John was not very communicative about his work, at least not to me. A huge man with dark hair and penetrating eyes, John had a charming personality and was very outspoken. Like Mark, everyone admired John, and the two men got along as if they were brothers.

Jane, on the other hand, was quiet and shy. She grew up in a very strict religious environment, and it showed in her entire appearance. Her beautiful naturally curly strawberry blond hair was always severely pulled back from her face. Sometimes it was pulled so tight, I wondered if it made it hard for her to smile. She wore long skirts and high necklines. No part of her figure was ever revealed, especially her breasts or hips. Beyond this austere facade was a very kind and loving young woman who never hesitated to do anything for anyone in need.

It was clear that John ran the relationship. I often heard his booming voice summon her, like a drill sergeant calling his company to attention. I knew that Jane would always acquiesce to John's immediate need, whether she wanted to or not, even if she was busy doing something else. She would stop everything and tend to him. Without her own driver's license, she depended on John for transportation. *No license!?!* I used to think, *Did they forget to burn their bras in Australia?!?* Not having her license was just another way for her to feel powerless. Though Jane made almost as much money as John, he was master of the dollar and doled it out as he saw fit. Furthermore, John made most of the decisions in their life. He was not what you would consider an equal-opportunity husband.

ALTHOUGH WE STRUGGLE FOR EQUALITY, WOMEN INHERENTLY FEEL LESS VALUED

JANE HELPED ME a lot during my pregnancy and after the baby was born. She provided the nurturing I couldn't get from my own family members who were halfway around the world. Jane and I came from very different backgrounds; still, we had an unspoken bond. We didn't hesitate when it came to helping each other. I would willingly pitch in to make her day and life easier. She did the same for me. On many occasions, I would encourage her to get her driver's license, particularly when John spoke adamantly against it. I encouraged her to go back to college and get her nursing degree. John said they couldn't afford it until he finished his own schooling, or whatever it was he wanted to do.

I thought it strange that Jane and I, who didn't have much in common, shared many of the same values about life. Mark and John appeared to be close, yet they didn't help each other in ways Jane and I did. How could it be that I knew what made Jane happy before John could figure it out? He had known this woman for years; he was her lover. But he was oblivious to her desire to grow and feel more self-confident. On the other hand, Jane instinctively provided the validation I needed. This was something I expected from Mark, my supposed best friend and partner.

Jane and I both wanted what our husbands had! We wanted them to treat us as equal partners; and we wanted more say in our lives. Jane and I hardly knew each other, yet we knew how to treat each other with mutual respect. Our husbands, who professed to love us, floundered in this department. Yes, Jane and I were the same gender, and we had empathy for each other. More importantly, I think, we were two people struggling for our own personal power and respect.

As party time drew nearer, Jane and I spent more and more time together. We talked little about the party. Rather, we discussed our fears, goals, disappointments, and desires. Most of our conversations revolved around our relationships, and the reasons our partners didn't seem to understand us. I thought, *What's wrong with this picture? Our needs are the same as theirs! Does being a woman mean we are less human?*

Although our situations were alike, in Jane's eyes, I was the stronger woman. When Mark and I argued, I stood up for myself and gave it right back. After all, I didn't have to ask his permission to get my driver's license, and I was already halfway through college. I wore what I liked and said what was on my mind. I had as much right to the family funds as Mark, although he thought differently. I felt like an equal partner, even if Mark didn't always treat me like one.

WE MUST FIND STRENGTH AND INSPIRATION IN OUR FRIENDSHIPS WITH WOMEN

THANKS TO ME, Jane began to assert herself. I was her inspiration, or so she thought. She sincerely wanted to be her own person, and, in her own way, she was equally inspiring to me. She was the first person, other than my mom, who made me feel proud to be a woman. Jane was not a small-minded person. She was not hurtful or judgmental. She was always available to help or just lend goodwill. Complaining was not part of her character; she just did what needed to be done with a quiet strength. All she needed was some encouragement to match this strength with her talent and abilities. We were compatible because where she was strong, I was weak, and vice versa. Both of us were nurturers, and we appreciated the fact that we had to work twice as hard as men to get the same attention and recognition.

Although I admired other women, I still suffered from a nagging jealousy toward them. It seemed that women were always in competition with one another for male attention. Jane's friendship was the first indication that I didn't have to compete with other women. I wanted her to get all the attention and praise she deserved because I was her biggest fan. She was truly an amazing, untapped reservoir of love, strength, beauty, and intelligence.

I have often heard women put down their own gender, and wondered, *How can they hate those people and still like themselves?* If we hate our own gender, we set ourselves up to compete with every member of it. We will never succeed in accepting our own wonderful gender qualities, and quite possibly never really like the opposite gender either. Instead, if we love our gender, it's easier to build truly great friendships and allow our partners to build friendships with the opposite sex without anyone feeling threatened. Furthermore, when we love our own gender, we can understand how someone else can love someone of the same gender. Consequently, we become more open and more tolerant of love between two men or two women.

This new admiration for someone of my own gender surprised the hell out of me, and I spent many nights trying to understand my new positive attitude toward women, and Jane in particular. The more I supported Jane's quest for self-esteem, the more self-confident I felt. *By helping another woman to build her confidence, I was indirectly building up mine, too.* The more I encouraged Jane to be herself, the more I felt my own inner strength.

On the day of the party, Jane and I discussed what we were going to wear. I had the reputation as the crazy American who wore provocative, hippie clothes, and I had no intention of disappointing our conservative Aussie friends at this final event. Actually, they secretly enjoyed my outrageousness and expected nothing less.

I had bought some new clothes for our trip home: the highest platform shoes I could find, bellbottom pants, and a dolman-sleeved sweater. It was a wild and very contemporary look that went with my new "do." I felt great! But what about Jane? She had no party duds. Most of her clothes were too dull and conservative for her newly found assertiveness. *Not good enough,* I thought. With a little encouragement, I coaxed Jane to get ready for our guests, and boy, were they going to be surprised.

It was an hour later when the doorbell rang and guests began to arrive. The music was loud; and the Fosters was flowing. To everyone's amazement, I decided to dress in an uncharacteristically subdued outfit and felt great about my choice. This *toned-down* me was so much more than a look; it was a symbolic gesture of friendship for Jane. It was her turn to have the spotlight.

But where was Jane? I hoped that she hadn't changed her mind or become afraid of her new assertiveness and returned to her former mousy self.

All of a sudden the room became quiet. Jane was standing at the living-room entrance, and all eyes were on her. Her hair had been released from bondage and a few curls bounced over one eye. Her form was so striking that at first, the details of her outfit were a blur. *Was that Jane's body?* Was that gorgeous figure always hiding under those unflattering clothes? Like a beautiful sculpture created with symmetry and contour, there Jane stood. Her breasts were visibly a part of her stature, and her legs showed their sinewy strength from years of walking to work and everyplace else. Finally, she looked as if she was actually proud to be a woman. The new Jane gracefully moved around the room as everyone stared in awe. Her face was dotted and dusted with only the slightest amount of makeup, which allowed her natural beauty to radiate. She wore a simple dress—one of mine (but in all honesty it never looked that good on me). She was stunning! She was the belle of the ball, and a surprise to everyone. But no one was more surprised than John. He stood and watched her, his face beaming.

I was proud of Jane and proud of myself. I didn't want to compete with Jane. I wanted her to be the most beautiful woman there. *But I'm not supposed to want other women to be more beautiful.* It was the first time I wanted another woman to have all the attention. My new way of thinking astounded me. I celebrated with Jane her new sense of self-worth and confidence. I was happy for her, not only for her beauty, but for her courage. She was on her way to becoming her own person. She overcame a major hurdle in her struggle for personal power, and her accomplishments helped me face my own hurdles with increased self-confidence.

WE MUST CREATE EQUAL ATTITUDES ABOUT OUR SEXUALITY

AFTER MY EXPERIENCE in Australia, I didn't need to compete with women for a man's attention. I certainly didn't like to hear a man make sexist remarks. I liked it even less when a woman made mean-spirited, sexist comments about another woman. I didn't like the fact that women were used as sex objects on screen or in advertisements, and worse, that women allowed themselves to be used as sex objects.

I know there are women who don't care to change their own sexist attitudes toward their gender. I feel bad that these women are still using male standards as a yardstick for their own value. I understand how terrifying it must be for some women to let go of generations of thinking that defines us as "dependents"—less able than men to take control of our own lives, never mind a company, or nation. Loving myself as a woman certainly doesn't mean hating men, and I don't have to put down men to feel better about women.

My experience with Jane taught me that we cannot build mutually satisfying intimate relationships if men and women feel trapped by opposing needs and desires and deeply ingrained sexist attitudes. In order for any individual to feel good about who she is, she must feel valued.

Men and women are brought up to feel like adversaries. But because we are now sharing more responsibilities in the home and in the workplace, we need to bridge the gap between the old way of thinking and today's reality! I know we are making efforts to try to balance our inequalities by offering opportunities to women in work, sports, the arts, entertainment, school, religion, and health. But why are we still reluctant to change our attitudes regarding sex?

When a woman truly values her sexuality, she is much more sexually confident and open to sexual pleasure. I have never met a person, male or female, who hasn't appreciated the idea of his or her partner enjoying and participating more fully in their lovemaking.

MEN AND WOMEN ARE MORE SIMILAR THAN DIFFERENT

LIKE MOST WOMEN, Jane and I had acquired the belief that women didn't want the same things men wanted. This concept has always been my biggest pet peeve. It's not that we are different, it's that boys and girls are brought up differently. And this supposed "difference" keeps women and men from being "equal."

I can accept the obvious physical differences between men and women, and even some of the hormonally induced, emotional differences, but these are few, and not as enormous as society makes them out to be.

Here are my reasons why *we are not from different planets:*

• Physically, our nerve endings aren't feminine or masculine. The nerve endings in our skin and genitals are made up of the same material. Hence, pleasurable sensations, including orgasm, are neither male nor female, and, therefore, are equally important.

• Emotionally, our feelings, such as sadness, happiness, anger, fear, and love are neither female nor

male. They are what they are—feelings! If we
bring up our daughters to believe that they feel differently from boys and must behave differently, we
are not telling the truth. We are setting up boys
and girls, men and women, to be enemies instead
of partners. Partners belong on the same team—
the human team.

Teaching boys and girls to like or want different types
of toys only helps to sell more toys. Teaching boys to hide
their feelings and not be like girls (heaven forbid!) denies
young men the opportunity to express themselves wholly
and enjoy their lives more fully. It also reinforces the erroneous notion that girls are weaker, vulnerable, and de-
fenseless.

Add to these misconceptions the different expectations
for girls and boys that help to promote sexism:

• Girls are told that they are weaker and are supposed to be concerned with their looks and bodies. Furthermore, they are not as sexual as boys, but
they are supposed to use their sexuality to attract
a partner. They aren't supposed to give in to their
sexual desires because then they'll be considered
loose, yet it isn't fair for them to tease the boys either. What's a girl to do?

• Boys, on the other hand, are supposed to be
bigger and stronger, and their sex drives should be
equally big and strong. They are supposed to score
in sex as they do in sports and are entitled to sex-

ual satisfaction. It's okay for boys to brag about their sexual experiences. After all, every boy wants greater *stud* status.

This kind of general sexism and inequality leads to sexual misconceptions:

1. Men have stronger sex drives.
2. Sex and having an orgasm are more important to men.
3. Women need love more than sex.
4. Women take longer to have an orgasm.
5. Men and women are too different to be compatible sex partners.

These are the most destructive sexual myths we are brought up to believe, and they are simply NOT TRUE. Our sexual drives are not hormonal; they are driven by passion. Sexual desire is a combination of physical and emotional factors and, as I said, men and women have similar physical and emotional traits. However, we are brought up to believe that because we look different, we feel and act differently; but believe me, we are more alike than we are different. Whatever differences we do have must be viewed as equal, not inferior. Otherwise, we are doomed to remain enemies rather than friends. Unless we begin to build a society of equal partnerships, the price we pay may be another century of broken hearts and failed relationships.

WOMEN ENABLE MEN
TO BE DIFFERENT, THEN HATE
THEIR SEXIST ATTITUDES

So if we are more alike than different as little girls and boys, what happens that changes us? Socialization. Why is it that when looking for something in the refrigerator, a man will not bend down any lower than the first shelf and will not move anything to look behind it. If it isn't in plain view, then it must not be there. So what happens? A woman comes to his rescue. She bends down, moves a few things, and discovers the buried treasure for which he was searching. Instead of letting a man fend for himself in the refrigerator, a woman enables his inadequacy by doing it for him. A man isn't born this way; he's trained by his parents' cultural attitudes.

Recently, my friend Tina's son was invited to the first wedding of his generation of friends. As the day drew nearer, Tina asked him, "Did you buy a gift yet?" "Not yet," was his response. So Tina went out and bought a nice gift and wrapped it herself for the newlyweds. She then gave it to her son for the wedding. After she had done this, she realized that she would not have gone through the trouble of buying a present if it had been her daughter who was invited to the wedding. We both agreed that by doing these kinds of things for our sons, we were intimating that a task such as buying a wedding gift is a female job.

These are not genetic traits; they are learned. When we give our children more opportunities to learn and share in all kinds of tasks, men and women will find more common ground on which to build, including sexual common ground.

Sexism Equals Racism Without the Color

John's attitude, as well as Mark's, was purely sexist. And years before I had the pleasure of living in Australia, I learned that sexism has no color, nor any border. Half of my family is African-American. Others are Caucasian. My stepfather is Native American, African-American, and Italian. If all my relatives stood together, we would look like a poster for celebrating diversity.

We all experienced some racism, but it was the sexism that went unnoticed. The black men in my family experienced their share of racial discrimination at school and work, so it amazed me to see these same men make sexist remarks to their wives and daughters. My white male family members had the worst attitudes. Although these men would fight anyone who made a racial slur to their black *brothers,* they didn't hesitate in making sexist slurs to their supposed *sisters.*

Of course, the female side of the family quickly pointed out this blatant hypocrisy, but the men were insensitive and resisted change. A civil war was brewing at home, and it was anything but civil. The female side of the family decided to boycott all (what the men called) "female duties." I can remember my mom explaining to my step-dad that "the party is over," and she was setting down some new rules of the house. The only man who didn't

have a problem with our female rights agenda was my gay
brother. He got it!

I'm happy to say that we were able to avoid a war and
negotiate changes in attitudes and behaviors relatively
peacefully. Well, actually we didn't really negotiate, the
women just stood their ground. We wanted the men to share
in household responsibilities, but even more, we wanted to
be treated equally. After all, we went to work, and our jobs
were as valuable to us. But I realized that before the men
could change, the women in the family had to change their
attitudes about themselves. The mens' attitudes were largely
determined and instigated by how we viewed ourselves. If
I didn't see myself as "chief cook and bottle washer," and if
I didn't act like one, it was harder for the men to treat me
like one. It also helped me to see how much stronger women
are when we all stick together. Not only were we able to
make the changes we wanted, we learned to bond at a different level that was more empowering than helping each
other clean up after dinner. We respected ourselves as
women, and our family life improved because everyone was
treated fairly. When I faced the inequality of Australian
family life, I knew there had to be a better way.

WE MUST LEARN TO BUILD COMMON GROUND THROUGH NURTURING EACH OTHER

IN SOME WAYS, I encouraged Mark's sexist attitudes
by nurturing his needs—doing for him, fixing for him, and

losing myself in the process. I felt that if I worked hard enough to make him love me, then our relationship would get back on track. Meanwhile, I resented him like hell for not appreciating me and my efforts to keep our partnership intact.

I'm a nurturer. I like to nurture others, and I'm able to do it effortlessly in almost all my daily activities. What does the word *nurture* mean to me? To help another person grow and thrive, physically, emotionally, intellectually, and spiritually.

Mark loved my ability to nurture him. And it wasn't just cooking and cleaning that he liked. Nor was it my drop-everything instinct to rescue him when he was looking for something in the refrigerator. He liked the encouragement I gave to his dreams, as well as the things I did to make his daily existence easier. But I was traveling down a one-way street. Mark would accept my nurturing and never return the favor—and I wondered why.

It's that socialization thing again. Mark, like most men, didn't have the knowledge or skills to nurture. We don't bring men up to be nurturers because we see that as a woman's role. I wanted more nurturing from Mark, but like most women, I freely and gladly gave encouragement and support yet felt guilty asking for it. After all, I was supposed to be the giver, not the taker. That's what I had learned. Sound familiar? Because I didn't feel that I deserved to be nurtured, I never could ask for it with conviction.

Since my life with Mark, I have become so much better at asking for and accepting nurturing from others. But to get to this point, I had to believe that:

• I deserved to be nurtured.

• It was good and healthy for my partner to have the opportunity to be the nurturer.

• I could teach my partner how to nurture me before any resentment or guilt crept into the relationship.

If I am nurtured during the day, my sexual desire flourishes at night. Great sex is a nurturing act. If one partner isn't doing his or her share of the nurturing, the imbalance will eventually topple the relationship. Every relationship must be committed to shared nurturing in order for it to thrive.

All of us can use some education in how to nurture, and we can teach one another using a hands-on approach, just like the way we practiced show-and-tell at school. In order to nurture our relationships, we must:

• Kiss each other with thoughts of nurturing.

• Tell each other that we are going to nurture our sex life with words and actions of encouragement.

• Touch each other with the desire to relax, not excite.

• Let sexual arousal come from each person's feeling of being nurtured.

• Build our partner's feelings of sexual self-confidence.

No ONE IS RESPONSIBLE FOR YOUR SELF-WORTH EXCEPT YOU

WITH MARK, I was using my giving as a means of getting, based on my fear of feeling unworthy, and my inability to stand up for my own needs. Instead of feeling loved, I just went deeper into my lack of self-esteem.

Ultimately, I had the mistaken notion that loving Mark would automatically make me love myself. Wrong! Women, as well as men, are so brainwashed into believing that when we fall in love with someone, that someone gives us a sense of self-importance. Or, if that someone sexually desires us, and we have a sexual experience with him, then we automatically will have the self-esteem that we so desperately need. This was another one of life's little myths that caused me great confusion and disappointment. By not feeling worthy of pleasure and believing that it was much more important to satisfy Mark instead of myself, I sabotaged any attempt to sexually satisfy myself, and I felt resentful. What I thought would give me a greater sense of security only made me feel less loved.

It is true that the love of a giving and caring person can help us feel better about ourselves. But, it's NOT that person's responsibility to fill our self-esteem hole. We are each responsible for our own life and how we make it worthwhile. No one has the right to diminish your value.

To expect someone to make you feel important is not the reason for a relationship. We can HELP to boost someone's self-worth, but we're not responsible for creating it or keeping it alive.

We all know we must take care of our hearts if we want to live healthy and long lives. We know we can't lose too much blood or we will die. Well, it's the same with our self-esteem.

Think of your self-worth in the same way you do your body. Imagine that you could turn the beating of your heart on and off with a switch. You wouldn't let someone else control that switch, nor would you give someone else the right to control any of your bodily functions. Neither should you give anyone the responsibility for the maintenance of your life or the right to make decisions regarding your emotional well-being.

It's the same with our sexual fulfillment. We are responsible for our sexual attitudes and how we choose to express them. No one can do your sexual homework for you; all you can expect is some help and encouragement. In the same vein, if all you're getting is discouragement and no help, demand more; or look for a true partner.

CHAPTER THREE

Sexual Self-Confidence Means Being Honest with Yourself

You're worth it!

SEXUAL BETRAYAL HAS TO DO WITH FEELINGS OF INADEQUACY

IT WAS 4 A.M., and Mark was still not home. I thought, *he could really be dead this time, or in the hospital. Where is he?! I can't do this anymore. It's killing me. I want this to work, but I can't live like this. Please come home, Mark.*

I heard some people loudly laughing outside my second-story living-room window. We lived in a small college town in Vermont, and it was summer. Usually there was very little noise, especially at 4 A.M., in our cluster of newly built apartment houses. I got up, and looked out the window. It was Mark and a few other people. He was in the back of a pickup truck with a blond woman, and she was snuggled up close to him.

It's over. As it says in the movies, "The End." There were no more chapters in this book. I felt sad but relieved. I remained calm.

"Mark?"

Silence.

"Mark?"

"Ya."

"Don't bother coming up."

I moved away from the window and walked over to the stove to make a cup of tea. I thought, *He'll probably come up anyway,* but he didn't. Instead, he rode off in the back of the pickup. I sat by the window and waited for the sun to come up, and for my eighteen-month-old daughter to wake up and give me a hug.

After two hours, Mark returned home.

"I didn't do anything wrong! Why are you so upset?"

He didn't do anything wrong! This was the second night in a row that he had stayed out without an explanation or apology. This was supposed to be our new start after months of separation. This was supposed to be the new Mark, the one who would be more giving and supportive of my needs and feelings. It had been a terrible past year, and now this.

How could he justify such hurtful behavior? Ever since Australia, Mark had changed. I wasn't Mark's friend anymore. I was his wife, and it was my duty to make his life easier. We were no longer on the same wavelength because we didn't value the same things. His freedom was the most important aspect of his life. His life. Not our life. I was in a one-way relationship going absolutely nowhere.

I sat in the kitchen and cried. I started to mourn the end of my marriage. Mark continued to yell at me.

"You're smothering me. Why can't I have some time with my friends without you always butting in?"

As usual, it was all my fault.

By now it was 7 A.M. on Sunday morning, and there was a knock on our door. I didn't think that we were being *that* loud. Mark answered the door. It was our landlord. He didn't even live in the complex. I thought, *Maybe we were too loud for Vermont.*

"I'm sorry to call on you so early, but your mother called, Susan, and she had an emergency message." Since we had no phone, I had left my mother the landlord's number in case of an emergency. "I'm sorry to have to tell you this. Your father died early this morning. Your mother said to be sure to tell you that it was your biological father, not your stepdad."

I got up and ran into Kyrsha's room to pack her clothes. Then, I rushed into my room to pack. Mark was behind me, frantically trying to apologize, panicked that maybe this time he had gone too far. I was going home *without him.* It was a very bad Sunday morning.

I was devastated. The news of my father's death and what I felt as Mark's betrayal brought to the surface all my childhood hurts stemming from my dad's rejection. I never felt loved by my dad. Hence, my biggest fear was being rejected by a man. And Mark's betrayal was the ultimate rejection. My dad was a dictator. He would order us around like soldiers, criticizing us about everything. As a

child, I so desperately wanted my father's love and validation but mostly got his anger and criticism. When I was
a little girl, my dad would reject and disown us kids on a
regular basis for any minor infraction. Of course, I took
his rejection personally and lived in fear of his leaving me
for good.

Here I was at twenty-three facing the same childhood
pain all over again. I had lost what little self-worth I had
and was completely shattered by this breach of trust. I tried
to tell myself that Mark's actions were his responsibility,
but the hurt little girl inside me kept nagging that it was
my fault, too. I fought my feelings of unworthiness every
day for months. To this day, I continue to feel pangs of
that same childhood fear of rejection.

Mark's sexual betrayal was like being blasted with a
gun. I felt a huge hole in the core of my self-worth. I felt
unsure of my value as a person, and I didn't trust my
thoughts or decisions about anything. The best thing I
could do was focus on my baby daughter and her needs.
It helped me to have Krysha because she depended on me,
and she was my reason for getting up to face each day the
best I knew how. Fortunately, I went home to my family where I was bathed in love and acceptance. If my husband didn't love and respect me as a valuable person, at
least my family did.

I needed to build my self-confidence with activities
that proved my worth and competence, but I still felt
shaky about trusting love and commitment from a partner. I realized that trust and honesty were THE corner-
stones of any and all relationships, especially between
parent and child. The legacy of my father's rejection had

to be acknowledged and validated if I was to move beyond my terror of being left alone or betrayed. I tried to
face the pain of my early past, but at twenty-three years
old, I could only dig so deep. I had some understanding
but few emotional resources. It took me many more years
to heal these childhood wounds.

PUTTING HIS NEEDS AHEAD OF MINE ONLY CREATED RESENTMENT

SEVERAL MONTHS had passed, and Mark and I were
living apart: he in our apartment in Vermont, and Kyrsha
and I with my mom. Mark had not yet told his family that
we were separated because he still believed I would change
my mind and get over IT—whatever IT was. He begged
me to go to Maryland with him for just a few days. He feared
that if he went home alone, without me and Kyrsha, his
family would be devastated. Reluctantly, I agreed. I loved
his family because they were so good to me and Kyrsha.

At his folks' house, I acted the part of the dutiful wife
and even slept in the same bed with Mark, but I told him
there would be no sex. "Our marriage is over," I said, and
I meant it.

On the way back home, Mark insisted we visit Rick,
his best friend from college, and his wife, Ann. We had
attended their wedding three years earlier but had not
seen them since our return from Australia. It meant that I
had to go through the charade one more night, and again
I gave in. I wondered why I kept making the same mis-

take. Once again, I allowed myself to be pressured into acquiescing to Mark's needs. I had little self-confidence to stand firm and make decisions based on my well-being.

Mark and Rick jumped right into their old routine: drinking beer and settling down on the couch to watch a baseball game. Kyrsha was asleep for the night, so Ann and I went to a movie.

On the way to town, Ann confessed that she and Rick were not as happy as they appeared. She needed something more in her relationship but didn't say exactly what. She was very confused about what she was going to do. I did not want to share my own separation story because I knew that this would probably be the last time I ever saw Ann and Rick. I didn't know Ann very well and always thought of her as a conservative sorority girl from Ohio. But, as she talked, I realized that Ann was not casual about life. Like me, she had a lot of unanswered questions and was desperately seeking her own power. She did not want to settle for being her husband's obedient wife and second-class partner. I knew exactly how she felt, but I sensed there was more. She wasn't sharing it, and I didn't press.

As we sat in the darkened movie theater watching a suspenseful, somewhat scary film, Ann became cold and physically upset. She covered her eyes and scrunched down in her seat. I put my arm around her to give her some physical and emotional warmth. I felt bad for her. She was so much more disturbed about her impending breakup than I was about mine.

Later, when we returned from the movie, Ann blurted out the whole truth about her problem. It wasn't that she wanted a better, or more equal relationship. She had fallen in love with someone else, and this someone else was a woman!

She waited for my response. So did I. Ann was in love with a woman. *Okay,* I thought, but still I did not react to Ann. She continued to talk about this woman—a wonderful, older woman with several children. Suddenly, she started to cry. I said, "Don't worry. Give yourself some time before you do anything. Talk to someone so you can be sure of your feelings. I don't think it's awful. She sounds like a nice person."

She was surprised by my somewhat muted reaction. I probably wasn't shocked because my brother recently had told me he was gay. And once, in high school, my best friend told me she was in love with me, and I remembered answering, "I love you, too." But my friend said, "No, I'm *in love* with you." That's when I freaked out. After all, I was only seventeen and the head cheerleader. I was supposed to be attracted to, and desired by, the football captain, and we all know how that turned out.

This time I did not freak out. This time, I was composed, and I tried to console a very distraught and scared woman.

The guys were still up, and in minutes, we all said good night and went to bed. Mark, filled to the brim with a twelve-pack of beer, pressured me to have intercourse with him. I reminded him that his chance at our marriage had ended. Moreover, I was angry at myself for getting talked into this visit, just as I was angry at his "entitled" attitude about having intercourse with me.

After a while, I heard Ann whisper at the door, "Please come downstairs. I'm very upset." I was wide awake myself, so I crawled out of bed quietly not to wake Mark.

Ann decided that she could not continue her sham of a relationship with Rick. He was nice enough, but her present desires pulled her in a completely opposite direction. We sat on the couch, our knees pulled to our chins so that we could get close enough to whisper. I realized that Ann was very much like me. Each of us was struggling for our individual identity, our sense of worth, and our own sexuality.

WOMEN HAVE LIBERATED THEMSELVES IN MANY AREAS BUT NOT AT HOME

Back in high school, it was so much easier. My boyfriend Gary encouraged me to use my power and treated me as his equal. Now that I was married, I was no longer an equal. Rather, I was treated like a piece of property. My needs always came second to Mark's. Even though it was a new era for women and our relationships, we still were expected to keep our place at home. Some outward things certainly changed, though: For instance,

1. We were no longer expected to remain virgins until we were married.
2. Many of us were single mothers, taking care of our children and spending our days out in the workforce.
3. More and more of us were going to college to get a degree, not just an MRS.

But although we burned our bras in 1970, we behaved as if we hadn't burned all those long-held, subliminal messages that kept us from acting equally in partnerships. The time had come for both women and men to change attitudes about marriage, expectations, and entitlement.

As I sat with Ann, I remembered other moments in my life with girlfriends who had been very important to me and had given me so much love, affection, and validation. At that very moment, I was suddenly overcome with a sense of empowerment. I wanted to regain the personal power I had lost at the altar. Ann and I both decided that we needed to gain some self-worth and strength so that we could follow through with some tough decisions. I said good night and went upstairs. I felt freer than I had in years: free to decide my own life course; free to be more of who I wanted to be; free to love myself without having to be loved by a man. Until that moment, I don't think I truly believed that women really were equal in value.

The next day, Mark went back to Vermont, and I went to live with my mom and stepdad. There was no more pretending that we were a team. Mark was right, after all. I wasn't his friend, and if I wasn't his friend, I didn't want to be his wife.

I never talked to Ann again, and I often wondered what happened to her. Mark and I have not talked in years. After we parted ways, he was married and divorced three more times. The one unfortunate result is that Kyrsha has continued to struggle with her relationship with her father.

SEXUAL SELF-CONFIDENCE STARTS WITH YOU

THAT EVENING WITH Ann opened my eyes about my feelings of worth. Part of what I learned was that I needed to be honest about my feelings. Seeing Ann's torment about expressing her true feelings showed me how much pain I was in, and how much I had tried to cover up what I felt inside.

Let this be a time for you to be honest with yourself. Let's explore and evaluate who you are sexually, how you view your body, what you think about your ability to be sexual, and how you express it. This exercise is not about value judgments. It's about discovering how and where you got your sexual attitudes. Once you uncover the source of your attitudes, it's so much easier to change them.

As you consider these questions, think about your life, from childhood to the present, and honestly examine your sexual development. If you want, write about the important moments in a journal. It can help you to understand the fear and shame you associate with sexuality.

1. WHAT ARE YOUR EARLIEST MEMORIES ABOUT BEING SEXUAL? Go back as far as you can, and try to remember any incidents that influenced your sexual feelings: playing with yourself, or friends, in a sexual way, or noticing any sexual images or feelings. One of my earliest

memories is from the time when I was six years old. My cousin, who was about twelve, was bouncing me on his lap when my sister walked into the room. She yelled at him for doing it. Then, she pulled me aside and told me that he was doing it to *feel good in a bad way.* "Don't be so stupid," she said. My sister was always quicker than I was to pick up on things like that!

2. WHAT WAS SAID TO YOU BY FAMILY MEMBERS ABOUT SEX AND MASTURBATION? This is important. Take some time to really think about how you got your attitudes about touching and pleasing yourself. For many of us, it was a negative message that has stayed with and still influences us. For me, it was: *How can I feel comfortable having someone else look at and play with my private parts when I haven't even seen them or touched them?* And to make matters worse, *If I do play with them, look at them, or even want to have personal sexual satisfaction, I'm a slut.*

3. WHAT WERE THE MESSAGES ABOUT SEX, SEXUALITY, AND YOUR GENDER'S SEX ROLE? Our self-worth is intertwined with our attitudes about gender. What did you learn about being a girl or a boy, and how do these attitudes influence you today? For me, the biggest message about being a girl was: Girls aren't supposed to be sexually assertive. This attitude carried over into other areas of my life, including work and relationships. I really needed to change this at-

titude so that I could help to create my own sexual satisfaction.

4. WHAT DID YOUR FRIENDS, SCHOOL, AND RELIGION SAY ABOUT SEX? Another biggie. I am a spiritual person and have studied many religions. I have learned that most religions are afraid to deal with issues of sexuality in a positive way. Promoting fear and shame only contributes to our inability to make sexual decisions. I began to feel at odds with my religious upbringing. All the religions of our civilization—Christianity, Buddhism, Taoism, Judaism, Islam, etc., were founded by men for men. Few religions, if any, allowed women to participate in the holiest and most sacred of ceremonies. All these male religious beliefs have had a powerful impact on me and on women in general. I knew in my heart and soul that these long-held beliefs were not true for me. If I continued to accept them, I would never be spiritually strong, which is what God intended all of us to be. And, for me, if a religion values a man's life more than a woman's, then it is not a true spiritual voice.

5. WHO DID SEXUAL THINGS WITH YOU THAT MADE YOU FEEL GOOD? Please take time with this one. We often forget our positive sexual experiences. One of mine was with my best friend, Diane. Many afternoons we would climb the three stories to my bedroom, crawl into bed

naked, and snuggle up to each other, pretending
to be lovers. We played boyfriend and girlfriend
and took turns being the boy even though neither
of us really wanted to be with a boy. At ten, we
didn't like boys because as we said, "They're
gross." As children, Diane and I loved each other,
and we explored in a way that never violated our
caring for each other. I remembered our time together as a sensual and loving experience. This innocent sexual discovery was connected to love
and friendship—two attributes many adults don't
value enough.

6. WHO DID SEXUAL THINGS WITH YOU
THAT MADE YOU FEEL BAD? These mem-
ories may be painful for some of you, and you may
want to talk about them with someone, like a
counselor, who provides a safe environment. I was
molested by a drunken family friend when I was
ten years old, and, trust me, I could not be as sexually positive as I am today if I hadn't talked about
this incident and moved through it.

7. WHAT WERE SOME OF THE MYTHS
AND MISCONCEPTIONS THAT YOU
LEARNED GROWING UP? HOW DID THEY
INFLUENCE YOUR SEXUAL CHOICES?
There were so many for me, mostly having to do
with a woman's sexual role—how we are sexually
satisfied, and how wonderful sex is supposed to be.
Men are encouraged to be sexually satisfied. That's

a good thing for them because it can help them become proud of their gender and their own sexuality. But I have to say that sometimes male sexual assertiveness can be too aggressive if it's expressed in a selfish or abusive way. Women, on the other hand, are still presented as less sexual and needing less sexual satisfaction. We are taught to hold off our sexual desires and use our sexuality to attract and control male attention. Women are supposed to resist and deny, and men are conditioned to go after and get. Once I understood the truth about women and sexuality, I had to revise the unclear messages and distorted images about sexual relations, especially intercourse.

8. WHAT SEXUAL INCIDENTS OR THOUGHTS ARE YOU STILL ASHAMED OF? If you feel guilty about anything, talk to someone. Try to understand the problem, and then make a plan to begin to change the situation. Give yourself the opportunity to clear a way for a new beginning. Take the time to face your sexual past so that you can create a better present, and look forward to a healthy future.

Self-worth and self-confidence start with the word *self,* which means you. The first step in creating self-worth and self-confidence is to make yourself a priority. You have to put time and energy into building your feelings of self-worth on a daily basis. And it doesn't come from the outside in. Although others can help bolster your confidence, you have to make every effort to be your first and foremost champion. You have to believe in yourself, and your talents and abilities. Regardless of what happens, you must be your own best friend, cheerleader, and coach. Above all, you must be your own nurturing parent.

NO ONE IS ENTITLED TO YOUR BODY OR YOUR GENITALS MORE THAN YOU

MARK CERTAINLY THOUGHT he was entitled to me and my body even when our marriage was over. He found it hard to accept the idea that my body was under my jurisdiction because he equated it with losing power. He also found it difficult to relinquish the belief that he had control over my life in general.

Like most men, Mark was taught that he had the stronger sex drive, and I was taught that I was the object and satisfier of that drive. However, *men are not entitled to women's bodies*. Women's bodies are meant for their own pleasure first.

Recently, I talked to a man about the top three purposes for a woman's breasts, in order of their importance. He agreed with number one: to feed babies. However, the next idea was a foreign concept to him. The second purpose for a woman's breasts is to give pleasure to HER. And the third is to give sensual pleasure to her partner.

"Wait!" he said. "How do her breasts give pleasure to her?"

I really didn't think it necessary to explain; it was so obvious to me.

"There are nerve endings in her breasts, skin, and hands, and when she touches herself, she feels pleasure. Exactly the way you feel pleasure when you touch your penis."

That should settle that, I thought. But, it didn't. He continued to argue with me about whether her breasts could really give her pleasure.

Then I got it! He didn't like the fact that women's breasts and genitals really belonged to women, and not to men. It was the order he didn't like, not the purpose. Her pleasure came before his. He was brought up to believe that a man was entitled to a woman's breasts even before she was. After all, aren't they used to sell everything? Aren't they used as the ultimate male turn-on?

This breast's for you! so the ad goes.

No! My breasts are for me!

It's time to balance the "entitlement scales." Until we do, men and women will always be sexually unequal. Any partnership is only as strong and as successful as the power of both individuals. If women are treated unequally, then partnerships will never find a firm footing. Women can bring as much, if not more, to their own sexual satisfaction when they believe they are entitled to do so. When women rely on men to take charge sexually, because they believe that men are more powerful or have a stronger sex drive, then relationships will continue to suffer. No one will feel satisfied.

Remember, every woman owns her body. No man is entitled to it.

9 HAD TO BE HONEST WITH MYSELF BEFORE I COULD BE SELF-CONFIDENT

BECOMING SEXUALLY PROUD and confident is a lifelong process that requires commitment and nurturing. It takes a lot of soul-searching and personal evaluation. It means we must examine long-held beliefs and be willing to adjust them to include correct information and new attitudes. To create a mutually satisfying sex life, each partner must truly look at his or her own blocks and fears that hinder the process and sabotage the result.

Ann's disclosure helped me to discover that for me, being honest with myself was a big obstacle to overcome. I had to admit that I was being dishonest with myself and Mark about who I was sexually, and what I needed from our relationship. I appeared to be sexually confident, relaxed, and satisfied, but underneath I was scared, uptight, and even faked orgasms. I couldn't admit that my physical sex actions were not honestly connected to what I was feeling emotionally. I feigned sexual knowledge and kept my spiritual life as far away from my sexual life as I possibly could. I was sexually dishonest with myself and my partner.

I lied to myself about many things, including the fact that I was using intercourse as a means to feel wanted and needed, to fill my lack-of-self-worth void so that I could feel important and desired. Using intercourse this way was not an expression of honest love and respect for myself or Mark. I tried so hard to deny my lie. I tried to outrun it, outsmart it, and hide it, but eventually I had to be honest with myself. I was a liar. I was being dishonest, and I had to stop. The lie wasn't about what Mark was not giving me; it was about what I wasn't giving myself. I wasn't giving myself the respect I deserved, and I was really angry at myself for being sucked into this cycle of dishonesty. If I didn't want Mark or anyone else to feel entitled to me and my sexuality, then I had to stop my participation in pretending it was okay. I lied about my sexual feelings, and I was the one lying to myself and my partner.

Once I admitted my dishonesty in my sex life, I was able to see other ways I was lying to myself about my career, my friendships, my parenting, and all areas of my life. It was the old, but faithful, snowball effect. I was thrown into a major spring cleaning of myself. Of course, the first emotion I felt after admitting my lies was shame, which at first only added to my lack of self-esteem. So, I had to do what every person should do when someone admits a mistake and is truly sorry for it. I forgave myself. I call it *sexual amnesty*. I truly forgave myself and promised to try never to lie to myself or anyone else again. I then took the next step to changing my dishonest ways and apologized to those I had lied to. Finally, I was beginning to feel happier about being a woman. I found a sense of power within me that enriched every area of my life.

- I stopped questioning my worth and my value. I knew I was capable of doing more because my self-esteem beat like a new heart inside my chest, pumping me up to do and be more.

• I stopped criticizing my body. All its imperfections were brushed from sight by my new self-loving attitude.

• I treated myself better because I truly believed I deserved better treatment.

• I celebrated my sexuality by not using it as an ego boost. I set my sexual goals at the same level as my emotional and spiritual ones.

CHAPTER FOUR

Masturbation Teaches Us How Our Bodies Work Sexually

What a relief!

WE HAVE TO TAKE OURSELVES AS OUR FIRST LOVERS

I WAS all alone. Mark and I were finished. I didn't have to pretend to his family or friends that we were still married. I was single again at twenty-five, a full-time college student, and the mother of an eighteen-month-old baby. It was summertime, and I was staying with my mom and stepdad.

Kyrsha was asleep in her crib, while I lay in bed next to the window, enjoying the stars and a cool New England ocean breeze. I had not had any sexual contact with

Mark or anyone else for almost a year. I felt my sexual tension rising, and I was confused and angry about it. Confused, because what the hell was I supposed to do with it. Angry, because I knew what Mark was doing with his sexual tension. For a while, we had a good sex life. He was a good lover and had a strong sex drive, and so did I. In Australia, we experimented with a vibrator, but I was afraid that John and Jane would hear the loud whine it made, or worse, the loud groan I made.

I always had orgasms during intercourse with Mark, but only if I was on top. Just as with Gary, I learned to stimulate my clitoris by sliding on Mark's erect penis, although his erection was inside me. Not that I remember calling it my "clitoris" then, but at least I knew my orgasms originated in that area. The experience was not much different from the one Gary and I had in his Volkswagen. I had to push down hard and slide back and forth awhile; but I was young and athletic, so it worked.

So, now what? I refused to go out and get "laid." Besides, I knew that I couldn't feel comfortable with a stranger, to ride him like a bronco for my own satisfaction. It had taken two years for Mark and me to feel at ease. No one-night stand could produce that kind of emotional and sexual safety. At least not for me.

The stars looked so bright that night. The cool ocean breeze tickled my skin, teasing me with its gentle touch, and I was about as sexually frustrated as a person could get. I remembered thinking, *There must be something I can do. Masturbate. No way!* Talk about embarrassing. *But, of whom am I embarrassed? MYSELF?!?* Oh, great, I'm embarrassed in front of myself. It was silly, and I started to laugh. None of my friends did it, or did they? We certainly didn't talk about masturbation, that's for sure.

Okay. I had to look at this idea logically. Intellectually, I knew masturbation was fine and normal. It was a viable option, and one that fixed the situation without putting me in any compromising situations. Plus, I didn't have to get out of bed, get dressed, go to a smoky, loud bar, meet a lot of drunken people trying to get laid, and end up in the backseat of some Camaro with a stranger. And, what if I didn't have an orgasm after all this? Not only would it have been a complete waste of time, but I would feel the worse for wear.

I always marveled at how quickly we took some stranger as a lover before we were able to be our own lover. I had learned that masturbation was worse than having intercourse with *a stranger*. How could this be? It was not logical nor did it make any sense.

Children take pride in learning how to do things for themselves. How many times have we heard a two-year-old say, "Me do it?"

I had so wanted to take this "me do it" approach when I was young, as I explored sex in the backseat of my boyfriend's car, but I was too afraid. Too afraid to take charge of my sexual satisfaction?! I certainly took charge of everything else at that time, including my choice of boyfriend. I knew that I wanted to express myself sexually. I had some idea of what felt good; yet, there I was, letting someone else make all the moves. Fortunately, I finally got smart and lay on top of him, so I could wiggle myself into an orgasm. However, the thought of touching my own genitals was perverted to me. *Give myself plea-*

sure? Would I have wanted Gary to brush my teeth, blow my nose, or take care of my toilet needs? No! So why would I let a stranger fulfill my sexual needs before I did?

I had to take myself as a lover so that I could accept myself and approve of my sexual desires. I had to learn to take control of my sexuality and had to let go of all the shame and guilt I had learned about masturbation. It meant that I had to treat myself with the utmost respect, and not let anyone else put me down or use me as a sex object. In other words, I had to learn to love myself before I tried to love someone else.

WHAT'S SO AWFUL ABOUT MASTURBATION? LET ME TELL YOU!

FOR ONE THING, it is . . . embarrassing. Why? Everyone makes fun of it.

Second, most religions say it is a sin. Forget that reason. My religion also teaches that to get divorced is a sin. In other words, my mother was going to hell for divorcing my abusive father; but my father, who was *not* Catholic, was getting a free ride to heaven! What a joke. Mom was a saint; Dad was an emotionally handicapped tyrant. That didn't make a whole lot of sense to me. Why should I believe their condemnation of masturbation? I didn't anymore.

Third, society says masturbation is for losers and people who can't find sex partners. I knew where to find a sex partner; I just didn't want one at the moment. I wanted an orgasm.

A fourth reason. Women aren't supposed to masturbate. Their need for sexual satisfaction isn't as strong as men's. I thought, *What's wrong with this picture? I have a strong sexual desire. Am I more male than female?* Or has this been one of the biggest lies stuffed down our throats. I must have touched myself as a child. I noticed my daughter grabbing her crotch every time I changed her diapers. She obviously enjoyed touching herself. I remember rubbing myself with my best friend Diane as a little girl. That must have been similar to masturbation.

So back to the first idea. It really must be my own embarrassment, and lack of experience, that's holding me back.

SEXUAL SATISFACTION IS NOT A GENDER PRIVILEGE

I WAS EMBARRASSED because I was operating under a major misconception. I had been told that women didn't need or want sex as much as men. Since my divorce, that theory had flown out the window because I was definitely sexually in need. I knew men who weren't embarrassed about masturbating.

That's because most men are usually brought up to *love* their private parts. I always say that guys are so fortunate in this one area. Sure, there is joking and teasing and embarrassment about size and the amount of "action it gets," but all in all, men are encouraged to feel proud of their manly parts. They are socialized to take group showers, pee in urinals together, and comfortably accept one another's

nakedness. It's a rite of passage to overcome genital shy-
ness and feel confident about their manhood. Of course,
not all men feel the same amount of comfort or the same
confidence about their penises, but at least society gives
men some encouragement, which in turn lessens embarrassment and increases male pride. I am still in awe of how
easy it is for most men to get naked, flop down on the bed
spread-eagle, and feel little or no embarrassment about it.

Women can certainly use more of this openness about
their womanhood. However, the experience of getting
comfortable with our genitals is a whole different ball
game. Few of us can ever remember seeing our own private parts as children or teenagers, never mind seeing
someone else's. We shower separately, pee in private, and
dress behind curtains.

Sexual satisfaction is not the exclusive right of men.
Sexual satisfaction is an attitude, and an attitude must
change before behavior can shift to support it. We have
to learn to love every part of ourselves and our bodies to
ensure pleasurable sexual comfort.

I remember when my daughter was in the first grade
at a private school. I was new and wasn't part of the scene
yet, but I wanted to get involved. I worked during the day,
so I couldn't attend the mothers' meetings which were
held on weekdays. Instead, I signed up for the fathers'
group which met on Saturdays when I was available. Anyway, I was much more skilled and experienced in the fathers' programs, such as fund-raising, sports, and fix-it
projects.

When I showed up for the first fix-it project meeting
(I even brought my own tools), I was told, "We really

don't have that much fun." I wasn't surprised. People usually say that when they want to exclude you from joining their private club.

It's the same with sexual satisfaction. Sexual satisfaction isn't an exclusive club that society has allowed men to feel more entitled to join than women. Orgasms are fun whether you have them by yourself or with a partner. And everyone is entitled to join this club. Masturbating is not an attack on your partner or your relationship; it's an affirmation of your right to be sexually satisfied. If you are in a relationship, don't hide the fact that you are seeking sexual satisfaction by yourself. You aren't cheating on your partner with yourself! Always tell the truth about your sex life. If your sexual routine doesn't satisfy both of you, then change the routine. If your partner won't change, then tell your partner you are changing your attitude and behavior. Sexual satisfaction starts with an attitude that celebrates the right to pleasure ourselves. And, just like my experience at school, we have to remember to bring our own tools!

But what were my tools? I made up my mind to find out. I didn't care what society or religion dictated about masturbation. It was my best option. I thought, *It can't be that hard. If guys can do it, so can women.*

Equality means having the right to masturbate and feeling sexually satisfied. If I can manage my own checking account, change my car's oil, start a career, and be a single parent, I could certainly take care of my own orgasm. Or could I?

By now, I had pulled the sheet all the way up to my neck and decided to do it. Where to begin? Maybe I should turn over and find something to rub, or I could just use my hand. *Oh, no! Not my own hand!* This was going to be more difficult than I thought.

I lay there thinking. *I let other people touch my crotch— several, as a matter of fact—and that didn't seem to bother me. Why is it so difficult for me to touch my crotch with my own hand?* I didn't know any of these people half as well as I knew myself. To be truly honest, I was uncomfortable and embarrassed when I did let someone touch me. I obsessed about possible odors or too much lubrication. Did other women have this much juice, and were they as embarrassed as I was?

So if I never felt one hundred percent comfortable with most of the "vulva touching" I experienced, it's no wonder I wasn't comfortable touching myself! I wasn't comfortable with any touching there. That's not to say that I didn't receive pleasure and satisfaction, but it was always accompanied by embarrassment.

9F YOU DON'T LIKE YOUR GENITALS, YOU WON'T BELIEVE ANYONE ELSE DOES

WHY IS IT that women have always seemed to be so ashamed of their bodies? I wondered when this shame and discomfort started, and why most women seemed to have so much more self-consciousness about their genitals than men. Mark was never ashamed of grabbing his penis, or having me grab it for that matter. It wasn't that penises are better-looking than vulvas, or nicer to touch. Why was it so difficult to handle my own genitals?

It's because I don't like my own genitals. That was the problem. Like most women, I thought they were gross. I couldn't rid my mind of all those comments about a girl's vagina smelling like fish that I heard in junior high school. I would cringe when I had to listen to all those terrible names used to describe the deep, dark hole between a girl's legs. It was humiliating and intimidating. I never knew how to respond.

Maybe I did smell like a fish! Maybe, it *was* gross down there. After all, there were douche bags hanging in some of my friends' bathrooms. I didn't know how to fight back on this one. I could never make fun of a boy's penis or testicles because I hadn't seen any yet! Besides, boys were proud of their private parts and made favorable comments about them. But girls never talked about theirs. My mother told me about boys' and girls' genitalia, but, in general, a girl's genitals were dark, secret places that no one was really supposed to know about.

Almost all of us can remember an incident from our childhood, a time when we noticed the difference between boys' and girls' private parts. You might have been playing in the bathtub, changing a baby's diapers, swimming naked, or, like my experience, going to the toilet together in first grade. It probably made an impression on you—especially the way it was handled by adults. You may have heard things like: boys have a "noodle" or "wiener" or "wee wee," or maybe penis; girls, well, girls don't have one. What? Girls don't have one! My first introduction to male/female differences was *girls don't have one!* What happened to it? Why don't we have one?

Through exploration, girls feel something there, but it is small and hidden. And, of course, no one offers to help us see what is there, or understand what it is. Eventually, we hear the word *vagina*. In my case, I thought they were saying, "bagina."

One little girl I knew couldn't say vagina; it came out "my china." Her grandmother thought this was cute. She used to say to the child, "Don't let the boys play with your china because they'll break it, and then you won't have anything to serve dinner on." Of course, this was funny to the adults, but it would set this little girl into a panic every time a dish broke. This same woman told her son to stop playing with his "doodle," or she would cut it off. This remark was usually punctuated with her waving a pair of scissors in the air.

These remarks may have seemed cute and innocent at the time, but to children, they start a process of thinking about sexuality based on fear and shame.

For girls, it seemed especially scary. We were teased about our vaginas, or the hidden place where the penis goes. I was in first grade when a boy told me that babies are made by putting a boy's pee pee in a girl's thing. Of course, I was horrified. I ran home in tears hoping that Mom would tell me differently. Much to my dismay, she confirmed the information. I said, "It isn't fair! I don't get a pee hose to play with and pee outside with. All I get is a hole where a boy gets to put his pee pee in." Nor did anyone ever say the word *urethra,* and teach me about *my* peeing apparatus, or said the word *clitoris,* and tell me it's made out of the same "stuff" a penis is.

We think kids can't understand the truth, so we give misleading and incorrect explanations, hoping that it will get easier when they grow up. It's a wonder we ever get this sex thing right at all. It's no wonder that many of my friends, female and male, don't like their genitals. I know this sounds ridiculous, and maybe you're thinking, "I can't really say I like mine, but so what?"

Sometimes, the people who love us know more about our genitals than we do, so it's really important that we get to know and like our genitals. Many times we reject oral sex pleasure because we dislike our own parts, their smells, or perceived bad taste. Our inability to watch our own lovemaking can come from being uncomfortable with looking at our own genitals. This is why so many women have a hard time masturbating. How can we enjoy a part of our body that we have been told to deodorize, powder, and flush out like a dirty sewer pipe? Masturbating can help us to appreciate our genitals and get over any shame-filled feelings that have been forced upon us.

Hating any part of our bodies greatly affects how much we like who we are as individuals. Hating the parts that we use for our most intimate and loving experiences limits the love and intimacy that can be shared between two people. We need to love our genitals just as we need to love ourselves.

WOMEN NEED TO KNOW HOW TO SEXUALLY STIMULATE THEMSELVES

I WAS STILL looking at the stars, waiting to begin my masturbation mission. An obvious dislike of my own vulva was apparent. I decided it was time to get over my lack of feminine self-confidence and self-worth. What would Gloria Steinem say? "Masturbate, young woman, and then run for president." Instead I said, *Okay, Suzi, be your own cheerleader. Your embarrassment can be overshadowed by your desire to be independent and proud of being a woman.* I was psyching myself. At the same time, I had taken some breaths and started to relax.

I closed my eyes because I still felt a little tentative and wasn't ready to watch yet. I gently lay my right hand on my panties. *Okay, I'm there.* I began to rub, searching for the exact spot that gave me an orgasm. I rubbed over and over again, getting a twinge of pleasure every once in a while. My mind started to wander, and I found myself thinking about what I had to do the next day. *Great!* I couldn't stay interested in my own lovemaking. I thought, *This isn't working.* I was ready to give up. Then I remembered what I did when Mark made love to me. I was thinking about SEX, and sexual things! I concentrated on his desire for me, and how great it felt to be loved. In fact, I was usually aroused even before he had touched me. My thoughts had anticipated the actual sensation. Yes, kissing helped, but before our lip-to-lip contact, I was usually wet and ready with desire.

I got it! It was my attitude more than the actual touch. My mind was in control even before foreplay began. I had to stop thinking about the stuff I had to do tomorrow and think about sexy things and making love with someone— anyone. I certainly could think of what it would be like. *Come on, Suzi, get into it!*

I started to rub other parts of me. I had some sexual arousal that night, but I didn't have an orgasm. Then again, I didn't stand up the first time I learned to water-ski, but I became rather skilled at it.

From then on, I continued to teach myself about my

own body and what I needed to bring myself to orgasm. I needed tender, gentle touching of my breasts and thighs, before I touched my clitoris. I had to think about a sensual and sexy encounter with someone. I liked wearing some clothes and slowly moving my hands underneath them, touching my skin.

Night after night, I kept getting closer to orgasm, discovering where I needed more pressure and exactly which areas had the most sensation. Soon, I discovered that my clitoris was more sensitive on the right side than the left. *Pretty good,* I thought, *considering the fact that my clitoris is so small, it barely has a right or left side.* I noticed, too, that if the hood or flap of skin that covered the small head, or glans, was pulled back, it was almost too sensitive to touch. Also, the more I got aroused, the more my clitoris and labia enlarged and hardened. *Sounds like a penis to me!* Instead of using my saliva, I liked my own vaginal lubrication because it was more slippery and helped to increase stimulation. The closer I came to orgasm, the more I could feel my muscles tense. My hand and fingers pressed down even more on my vulva. I was sweating, and breathing heavily, and my vagina and uterus throbbed. This was different than having intercourse, or sliding up and down on Mark's erection. It was actually more intense. My clitoris, and my whole pelvic region, felt on fire.

I continued rubbing, making sure I touched the right side of my clitoris. My whole body felt as if it were turning to stone, as my muscles hardened with an anticipated explosion. This was going to be the night! I wanted this orgasm—not just for sexual release, but for my own independence. I wanted it for self-esteem and for my sexual freedom.

My arm and hand started to tire, and I was soaking wet. *No stopping now!* I was determined to *go all the way* this time. I hung on to the edge of orgasm, for what seemed like hours, but in reality was only a few minutes. I kept telling myself, *Relax and let the pleasure come. I deserve this orgasm and this pleasure. After all, it's my body; these are my genitals; and I need to be in charge of them and enjoy them.*

I gave a few more rubs directly on that hard and swollen piece of flesh called my clitoris, and let it lead my pelvis and the rest of my body into a very intense and long-overdue, but deserved, orgasm.

I didn't know what felt better—the actual orgasm, or the feeling of accomplishment. Unfortunately, there was no one with whom I could share this newfound success. How frustrating! I had just learned to masturbate, and I couldn't even brag about it.

So there, Mark! You can take your pickup-truck honey and stuff it. I don't need your bullshit or your lack of support to get my needs met.

UNDERNEATH THOSE FUNNY-LOOKING BODIES, OUR GENITALS ARE VERY SIMILAR

I LEARNED A LOT during those masturbation exercises, but the most significant thing I learned was that men's and women's genitals are alike even though they don't look alike.

In the womb, the genitals of all fetuses start out as feminine. By the third month or so, male genitals begin to show for the boys, but the nerve endings have already been formed for both males and females and remain the same for life. The major concentration of these genital nerve endings is located in the penis for the boys, and in the clitoris for girls. So, our orgasm centers are located in the exact same places, on the outside of our bodies.

For men, the nerve endings radiate to the scrotum, testicles, anus, and base of the penis, but the most potent concentration of nerve endings is located at the end of the penis, in the first two inches, called the glans. The rest of the penis is there to hold up the very important first two inches!

For women, it's the same. The largest concentration of nerve endings is located in the clitoris, located just above the vaginal opening, similar to the place of a penis. The nerve endings radiate into our labia, anus, the opening of the vagina, which is called the PC muscle, and inside the vagina.

Aha! Men and women have sexual pleasure centers in the same place on their bodies, and we all need some rubbing and touching on these places to guarantee an orgasm. We also have similar emotions and the same need to be loved and respected. The more alike we realize we are, the easier it is to find and build compatibility.

I AM RESPONSIBLE FOR MY ORGASM, AND YOU ARE RESPONSIBLE FOR YOURS

GREAT! I learned how to sexually satisfy myself. It took a while, but I did it. I also learned to like my genitals. They worked well; they brought me pleasure; they weren't gross; and they didn't smell as bad as everyone said. Come to think of it, how come I don't hear men being teased about their genitals not smelling too great?

I must have practiced masturbating every chance I got. I stopped only when my clitoris was too sensitive to touch, when I felt uncomfortable in my jeans. I still had some shame and embarrassment, but I was getting over it.

My masturbation revelation led me to yet other sexual attitudes that I needed to explore: Was sexual release more important for men? Did women need to masturbate as much as men? Masturbation didn't change all of these attitudes immediately, but it was another tile in my newly laid sexual foundation. I needed to challenge any sexual attitudes that didn't help me become more sexually self-confident and satisfied.

For instance, I always thought a man was in charge of my orgasm. I knew I had to help, but in some way, I believed orgasms were part of sex with a man—either in him, or on him. And even though I could have orgasms during intercourse, I felt there was something not quite right with me when I couldn't have them while lying on my back.

GIVING YOURSELF SEXUAL SATISFACTION IS LIKE GIVING YOURSELF A PAT ON THE BACK, ONLY A LITTLE LOWER

ALL IN ALL, I had a new picture of masturbation. It wasn't something to do when I couldn't get a partner. And

I felt relieved that I didn't have to opt for one-night stands where there were no guarantees that I'd have an orgasm anyway.

What was all the fuss about, anyway? Masturbation didn't make me more promiscuous. It didn't make me a sex maniac. It didn't lure me to orgies and perverted sex parties. I didn't feel as if I were doing anything against God or another human being. I was giving myself pleasure. I was making love to myself. I was learning to take care of myself sexually, the same way I take care of my teeth, clothes, face, body, hair, bills, homework, daughter, car, and everything else that belonged to me and was my responsibility. It was another way to express my sexuality and a commonsense approach to sexual satisfaction.

How many times have we all wished that someone we cared about would give us a compliment—or told us that we did a good job, or that we're great and much appreciated? It's a great feeling, and one that we don't get to experience enough.

Why is giving ourselves sexual satisfaction any different? A compliment is a compliment, even if you're giving it to yourself. I feel the same way about masturbation. It is a compliment you give yourself, as if you were saying:

I like you, and I love you. You are worth loving, and you deserve sexual caressing and touching. I love making love to you, and I am not ashamed to admit it. I will do what you like and not judge it as bad or deviant.

We wouldn't hesitate saying something like this to our partners. So why would we treat ourselves any less lovingly than we would treat our partners?

MASTURBATION IS NOT A FOUR-LETTER WORD, SO DON'T TREAT IT LIKE ONE

ACTUALLY IT'S eleven letters. Okay, I MASTUR-BATE. There, I said it. And nothing bad has happened to me. I am still a good and moral person. I am still a good mother. I am still very much in love with my partner, and we still have a great sex life.

We've all been made to feel guilty and ashamed of masturbation, but it is a healthy outlet and expression of our sexuality. We've been taught to be dependent on someone else, a stranger, to learn about our own bodies and how they work. Some of us think that we're broken because our partners will never discover our pleasure centers, or worse, not care! All we have to do is give each other permission to discover how we have an orgasm—how we receive pleasure from ourselves. This is such a simple, yet integral, aspect of sexual confidence and satisfaction.

Like most young people, I actually believed that having intercourse with someone else, before I was ready, was better than masturbating. Where did I get that idea and attitude? From every movie, romance novel, television soap opera, and advertisement that used sex to sell everything, from drain cleaner to a new car. As forward-thinking as Mom was, she never said: "By the way Suzi, it's okay and better to learn to sexually satisfy yourself before you have intercourse. It's all right with me if you masturbate." I wish she had. Then again, I didn't say that to my daughter. However, when Kyrsha was twenty, I encouraged her to explore this area of her sexuality, and she did. A few months later, she was successful—she had an orgasm! No matter how great her sexual relationships are or will be, it was still important for her to discover how to please herself.

THE HISTORY OF MASTURBATION, OR HOW WE WERE DECEIVED

SO WHY AND where did this aversion to learning how to sexually satisfy ourselves come from? Well, let's look at the history of masturbation. Even though it's not a high-school or college course requirement, I'm sure if it were offered, this class would be filled every semester.

As a religious civilization, we figured out that by controlling a person's sexual attitudes and behavior, we would have power over much of his or her life. Furthermore, the easiest way to control attitudes is through fear, shame, and guilt.

It's not so surprising that without the right information, myths about sexuality were developed as a means to control people's behavior. Of all the sexual acts, masturbation was the first one to be attacked and repressed. During the Middle Ages, the Church forbade masturbation and deemed it as most sinful. St. Thomas Aquinas denounced it because it did not produce children.

At various times in our social evolution, masturbation was blamed for causing a myriad of miseries such as: skin disease, epilepsy, bed wetting, round shoulders (I guess this happens only if your arms are too short to reach your genitals), blindness, depression, insanity, tuberculosis, asthma, rheumatism, stomach cramps, impotence, hairy palms, rickets, loss of vitality, hysteria, and suicide. How did they miss crooked teeth?

In the eighteenth century, Swiss physician S. A. Tissot said that semen was man's most vital fluid and that wasting semen (via masturbation) drained the body of vitality and left it susceptible to disease. There goes that disease scare again. A surgeon from America agreed with Tissot and was so against masturbation that he developed a breakfast food that he believed would lower sex drive. The surgeon was Dr. John Kellogg, and his breakfast food was corn flakes. Dr. Kellogg also recommended sewing up the male foreskin with silver wire to make self-pleasuring painful. For women, he advised burning the clitoris with acid.

Anyway, this campaign against self-satisfaction did not end there. By 1940, we were no closer to tolerating masturbation; a Naval Academy midshipman could be thrown out of school if caught masturbating. I guess if you got caught, you were considered too stupid to serve in the Navy. And if you thought the medical community was more supportive of our natural urge for sexual satisfaction, think again. In 1959, over half of all medical students believed that masturbation caused mental illness, and that's because so did one in five of the medical faculty.

Unfortunately, our attitudes about masturbation have not matured. We are still too quick to make fun of it and giggle with embarrassment when the subject is raised. Most recently, our surgeon general was fired for ac-

knowledging masturbation and suggesting that it be discussed openly and factually as part of our children's sex education.

In case you don't know, masturbation doesn't cause
any diseases. Yet, we still continue to have myths about
masturbation. They are as follows:

- It's only for those who are not able to find partners.

- Mostly men do it.

- If you masturbate, and you have a sex partner,
your relationship is in trouble and you're not getting satisfied.

- Masturbation isn't real sex.

- Masturbation leads to sexual perversion and an
uncontrollable sex drive.

All these are false. If some people are not satisfied with
their sex lives and masturbate secretly, or do not tell their
partner, the problem is not masturbation but a relationship that is not based on mutal honesty. There are some
people who use masturbation in unhealthy ways, but that
doesn't make the act bad. It is a sign that these people still
have unhealthy sexual attitudes. Masturbation, like any
sexual behavior, or nonsexual one for that matter, can get
out of hand (pardon the obvious metaphor). In fact, the

problems that occur with masturbation usually happen because of the unspoken shame and guilt it evokes. Some
people might have emotional problems, and they use masturbation in a less than healthy way. But, for most of us,
it's a natural, healthy sexual expression.

$\mathcal{T}$HE GOOD NEWS
ABOUT MASTURBATION

NOW THAT WE have explored the bad news about
masturbation, here is the good news:

• It teaches us how we work sexually, how we
reach orgasm in a safe way so that no one can take
advantage of us or use us for his own sexual satisfaction.

• It helps us to appreciate our sexuality and genitals and not to be overly embarrassed or afraid of
our sexual feelings.

• It teaches us to take responsibility for our own
sexual satisfaction.

• It helps us realize that we are all similar in our
sexual needs and, at the same time, different in our
sexual likes and dislikes.

• It helps to relieve sexual tension and emotional
stress. It produces endorphins which make us feel

more satisfied and relaxed. This feeling of well-being also helps strengthen our immune systems.

• Masturbating to orgasm keeps our genitals healthier and stronger for our later years.

• Women who masturbate require less time to get aroused, have more orgasms, greater sexual desire, higher self-esteem, and greater marital sexual satisfaction.

Are you surprised by this new positive look at masturbation? We can change our attitudes about a sexual act that has such a long history of negativity and shame, but it takes time and a commitment. Explaining about masturbation to someone you love is not as difficult as you might think, especially if you believe it is a healthy sexual expression. That's the key. Let's bring masturbation out into the open, and discuss it honestly and with respect as a valuable part of sexuality. Masturbation is not a horrible and demeaning substitute for intercourse. It's a private, sexual expression that needs public support and understanding. It's a valuable sexual act that builds self-confidence and self-esteem.

9 NOW KNOW HOW I WORK. DO YOU?

RESHAPING MY ATTITUDE about masturbation was one of the single most important changes that helped to bring me closer to becoming sexually proud and confident. It was a step toward self-reliance. I had to rely on myself for sexual satisfaction. I didn't do it out of bitterness or resentment, or because I was single. Those issues may have encouraged the exploration, but they did not fuel it. I masturbate because:

1. I know the location of my clitoris, and where it likes to be rubbed and touched.

2. I know where the pleasure areas are in the most hidden parts of my body.

3. I know what I need sexually during different times of my emotional ups and downs.

4. I know about the opening to, and the inside of, my vagina.

5. I have felt my vulva harden, filling up with blood, as my excitement level increases.

6. I know how and when my juices flow and change in consistency during my menstrual cycle as my hormones fluctuate.

7. I know that stress and an overtired body can block my sexual desire.

8. I know what it takes to get me to concentrate on my pleasure.

9. I can recognize different kinds of orgasms and enjoy each one for its own uniqueness.

I realized that I liked giving myself an orgasm and taking myself as a lover. I will for the rest of my sexual life.

CHAPTER FIVE

We All Need Love and Acceptance More Than Sex

And you don't need to be a doormat to be loved!

KNOW WHAT YOU WANT, THEN ACCEPT NO LESS

IT WAS A BEAUTIFUL New England evening. The summer seemed to be filled with them, or maybe I was just more appreciative of them in those days. I was home for summer break, but unlike most of my college class-mates, I wasn't out every night partying with my old high-school friends. I didn't even know where most of them were. It had been six years since I graduated from high school, and my life had changed quite a bit. I don't know what I would have done without the love and support of my mom and stepdad. They had a beautiful, loving relationship. They adored Kyrsha, and I learned how important grandparents are, not only for the grandchild's emotional well-being, but also for my well-being as a single parent.

I left Kyrsha with her doting grandparents and took a walk to the community drug and alcohol self-help organization. I wanted to see if my volunteer application had been accepted. How strange it was to be at Turnaround House again. A bunch of my friends had started this organization several years before as a drop-in center for kids with problems. Since then Turnaround House had developed into a real service center dealing with all sorts of community problems. It had a great reputation for truly making a difference in people's lives. I knew a few of the people working there, but the chief administrator was new to me. He was the main reason why this center had grown to be one of the best nonprofit social-service organizations around Boston, and I wanted to meet this miracle man.

His name was Jake; he was charismatic and very smart. Everyone loved him and admired his ability to build a team out of the most unlikely and diverse individuals. From politicians to long-haired hippies, Jake brought people together. They put aside their differences to do some good for the community. He was the perfect mediator. His longish hair and beard helped to calm the young, and his neat, preppy clothes and skilled business sense reassured the town elders that city funding was being well spent.

During my brief interview, I was completely taken with Jake. Not in a sexual or flirtatious way, but with his energy and commitment to the program and his staff. He was a driven man, a leader on a mission. He was also very attractive. But I was much more interested in what I could learn from him, and that I could spend my summer doing something positive and worthwhile.

On my first day as a volunteer, I was told to stop by Jake's office. He greeted me with a robust "Hello," as if I were his long-lost friend whom he was truly happy to see. Again, I was captivated by this very special man, only this time the feeling was ten times more intense. Jake said he would like to get to know me. He felt that I would be a very important asset to the program.

The night shift was arriving to answer the hot line. Jake invited me to the neighborhood pizza parlor to meet a few of the employees who were already there. I was thrilled. As we walked across the street, he asked about my family, and I told him I was divorced and a single parent. He was also separated and had a stepson. We talked about parenting and all the difficulties of painful separations.

We shared pizza and beer with the other employees of the center. It was more a family of friends than merely employees. I watched Jake all through dinner. He was attentive to everyone at the table and joked with them like no boss I had ever known. Jake relied on his very outspoken and tough female administrative assistant, Sheila. She had outstanding business expertise, and he always deferred to her assessment of budgeting problems. Between slices of pepperoni and mushroom pizza, Jake and Sheila decided on several financial strategies that would save much-needed and important services. I could see that he truly respected this woman's judgment and credited her contribution to his success. I liked this fellow who gave recognition to his workers and remained humble. I liked him a lot!

Jake and I walked home. I sensed that he might be interested in more than my volunteering skills, but I didn't mind. Our attraction for each other increased with every step. As we slowly sauntered down the brick sidewalk streets, we discussed a variety of personal issues, ones that I hoped someone like him would understand and accept.

It was late by the time we reached my place. The temperature was still hot and the air muggy. "Would you like to come up and have a glass of lemonade before you go home?" I asked. It sounded so corny, but I did have fresh lemonade in the fridge. He responded, "That would be great." As we climbed the stairs to my parents' two-story apartment, I told him, "We have to be quiet because everyone is asleep." I felt like a high-school girl hanging on to her date for a few extra minutes before he had to leave. Only now, I was twenty-four and had a baby in the next room. We peeked into Kyrsha's room. She was curled up in one corner of her crib, little drops of sweat shining on her wisps of baby hair.

We sat in the kitchen drinking lemonade, still talking about our lives and future goals. I was feeling happy and so stimulated by this charming man. Then, an awkward silence fell—the kind that gives you an opportunity to regroup and decide if you're going to risk getting deeper into the attraction. Jake spoke first.

"I know this may be a bit presumptuous, but I really enjoy your company and would like to get to know you better. I'm going camping this weekend to meet some old friends. Would you like to go?"

I was thrilled that he had asked me. I quickly said, "Yes!" I offered my cooler and other equipment to add to the weekend's comfort.

Then as fast as I said "yes," I stopped mid-kitchen, the cooler stuck to my arms. I thought to myself: *What are you doing?* I had forgotten something very important: I did not want to have an affair.

DON'T SACRIFICE YOUR SELF-RESPECT FOR A ROLL IN THE HAY

BEFORE I MET JAKE, I had done a lot of thinking and soul-searching and had come to some conclusions. I didn't want to go out with someone merely as a casual encounter. It was okay to date, but as far as having intercourse was concerned, I wasn't into *the sleep-and-run* syndrome. Although it was 1974, and free love was the national youth anthem, I couldn't handle it. At least I knew that about myself. I wanted a relationship. I wanted to spend time with someone who also wanted a relationship.

This wonderful man was asking me to go camping, and I had said "yes" before thinking about it. I figured I could go anyway, and see what happened. Maybe, he was looking for a relationship, too. Or, I could tell him how I felt. I could tell him I was interested in finding someone who would like to have a long-term, committed relationship. I could just come out and say it!

What? Am I nuts? I just met this man. He'll think I'm a wacko. No! Worse! A husband-hunting female. I'll scare him away. He'll think I'm a needy woman who's looking for someone to take care of her.

Wait a minute! I didn't need someone to take care of me. I had my own money, home, and car. I was taking care of my daughter and going to college full-time. I simply didn't want a casual fling. The cooler was beginning to bond with me. I was afraid to put it down and face my decision. I would either go, and ignore the commitment I made to myself, or I would explain my position and see what happened.

I decided to take my chances and let this man know who I was and trust he was of the same mind. I would love to go camping, but I needed to be honest with him. More important, I needed to be honest with myself.

Jake just stared at me. I must have looked like a television stuck on vertical hold. I smiled and gave myself an emotional smack to the side of the head. When I finally put down the heavy, empty cooler, I began one of the most difficult explanations of my life:

"Jake, I really want to thank you for inviting me to go with you. I haven't been camping in years, and I bet your friends are great people. I need to tell you something that's a little awkward for me. [What an understatement!] I've been doing a lot of thinking since the breakup of my marriage, and I now know what I need and what I'm looking for. I'm not good at . . . Wait! Let me put it out there plainly and simply. I'm not interested in having an affair. I'm looking for a long-term relationship, and I wanted you to know this. I didn't want us to get close without your knowing where I'm coming from right from the start. I know what I'm saying sounds weird, especially over our first glass of lemonade, but I need the practice. I just felt that you, and I, deserve to hear out loud the commitment that I've made to myself. No affair. I will really understand if you'd like to ask someone else to go camping with you, and you can still use my cooler."

I did it! I explained exactly what was on my mind, and I didn't keel over! Actually, I felt great and proud of myself. Jake looked a little confused. As if I had X-ray vision, I could see his brain processing what I had just dumped on him. I was prepared for his backing out of the offer, judging me as an intense female who says too much of what's on her mind, too soon, and with too much honesty.

Yup! That's what I was all right, and I wasn't going to apologize or deny it any more. My lack of assertiveness and fear of going after the equality I needed had only served to end my marriage. From now on, I was traveling a new course, one that included my goals and my self-worth. I thought it better that he know who I was before we crawled into that cozy tent together, and I really did mean it about the cooler.

Jake took a breath, and I calmly waited for his verdict. I was ready to accept whatever happened. He started to smile and shake his head.

"I knew from the first moment I met you in my office that you were someone to be reckoned with. I just didn't know how much. I really appreciate your telling me all this. I guess it took me by surprise. I'm not used to someone coming right out and being so honest, but it's refreshing. When I asked you to go camping, I guess I was just thinking about the weekend. Now that you bring it up, I need to think about where I'm going in terms of relationships, and what I want."

He paused and looked at me before he began to speak again. I looked at the cooler and felt as if it were a container for my newly found risk-taking honesty instead of Mom's potato salad.

"Ya know, Suzanne, I don't want an affair, either. I am much more interested in having a relationship—one that has the potential for a long-term commitment. So would you like to go camping with me this weekend?"

His smile was so big, it lit up the room. We went camping and had a great time. Jake and I spent the next five years together.

SOMETIMES WE HOLD BACK THE TRUTH TO AVOID REJECTION

I WILL NEVER forget that night in Mom's kitchen. It was a turning point in my struggle for self-worth. Even though Jake and I didn't spend the rest of our lives together, it was an auspicious start in the right direction. One of my greatest struggles had always been caring about my partner's well-being to the exclusion of my own. I liked being a nurturing person, but I was a hypocrite to deny and ignore my own need to be nurtured. I wondered why I had little trouble sticking up for someone else's interests and so little concern for my own. This imbalance didn't make me a more loving person; it made me a *needy* person. I gave and gave, hoping to get back. I allowed an unequal relationship to go much too far before I spoke up for myself.

Telling myself the truth turned into a twenty-five-hour-a-day job, and at first, seemed more scary than rewarding. I stumbled and fell a few times and had to go back and admit where I'd messed up. I can remember slipping back into my old "acting honest habit," only to stop, sometimes in mid-sentence, excuse myself, and restart my sentence with honest words. No one could "act" more honest than I. I could say all the right words—the ones my partner wanted to hear. I could make believe all was fine when in fact I was miserable. I was capable of saying what needed to be said to make everyone else happy and content, knowing damn well it wasn't what I wanted or needed. I was a great "acting honest" actress. I even started to believe my own lies, and believing my own "act." I did all this acting because I was terrified of facing the truth and even more afraid of implementing it. And the truth was: I had let my relationship become a place where my partner thrived while I floundered.

Being honest with myself was hard enough, but being honest with my partner was even tougher. But once I was honest with myself, being honest with my partner got easier. Expressing my sexual fears and insecurities to myself first made it more comfortable to share them with my partner. Of course there was no guarantee that my partner would react the way I would like. BUT . . .

Love and respect come with an obligation to tell the truth to your partner. The biggest block to telling your partner the truth is fear of rejection, fear of being left alone or less loved. This fear, no, this terror, is understandable, but it can never justify lying. Believe me, I know. I've tried. Lying to your partner is like putting a crack in a building's foundation. You'll never know what might cause it to topple, or when it will happen. Maybe it never will, but you live with the constant fear and threat that it might. You can never feel totally safe, and your partner will *sense* that something is not quite right. This *sense* shows up as a small, nagging mistrust or insecurity about the intensity of the love professed.

HOW NOT TO RELATE WITH EACH OTHER

SO MANY TIMES we have sex before an emotional foundation has been created between partners—before either person really knows what the other one is thinking and feeling about a possible relationship.

- We are so afraid to say the true words, the ones that explain honestly who we are and what we believe.

- We maneuver ourselves and our needs so they will appear to fit our partner's.

- We force and pretend compatibility before we know if there are any real similarities or common ground.

- We make ourselves believe that sex will *create* the emotional foundation that's missing.

- We change or ignore what we truly need in order to make a connection—one that may never have any potential in the first place.

• We kid ourselves into believing that *when I feel safer, I'll start to be more honest with my partner.* The flaw or fallacy of this idea is: dishonesty, even the slightest speck, doesn't create a safe environment. In fact, it does just the opposite.

Once you lead your partner to believe you're a certain way, or like certain things, you'll be more reluctant to show him or her the real you.

IF YOU CAN'T TELL YOUR PARTNER WHAT YOU WANT, HOW YOU WANT IT, AND WHERE YOU WANT IT, YOU'RE NOT READY TO WANT IT!

IN SPITE OF MY initial honesty with Jake, I can remember doing sexual things with him before I was able to talk about doing them.

Why don't we take a commonsense approach to sex as we do to most things? Before we do a job, we talk to the person who wants us to do the job. When we go out with other people, we talk with them about where we're going. When we play sports with others, we talk about how we're going to play, and who is going to do what—it's called teamwork. When we take our car to the mechanic, we talk about what needs to be done, and how long it will take.

When we go out on a date, we talk all night, about work, family, movies, restaurants. But the minute we start kissing, all talking stops!

If we are too embarrassed to talk about our emotional needs and what we want and don't want to do sexually, we ought to be far too embarrassed to do it!

IF YOU CAN'T SAY THE WORDS, DON'T DO THE DEED!

I so wanted to let my potential partner, Jake, know who I was right from the start. I wasn't going to be sexual with a new partner because we both liked to go camping. I wasn't going to dilute my desires just to get into a tent with this man. I used to think that liking myself was never as important as liking someone else and having him like me. As much as I wanted to be needed, I needed to learn to ask for what I wanted. In retrospect, it was a small step on my journey, but monumental in its significance. I risked being rejected, which was one of my biggest fears, in order to take a stand for me.

I started my encounter with Jake with honest communication. That in itself was a major turn of events. I didn't follow my usual routine and merrily go along until I felt comfortable enough to say what I truly thought and felt. I made a definitive and true statement (in a positive way, I might add) about what I needed. I let Jake know, without hurting his feelings, that I didn't want a momentary sexual tousle in the tent.

In the past, I was always afraid to say what I wanted. I would have felt guilty for standing firm for me at the risk of losing him. The bizarre thing is, I felt like this only in love relationships with men.

In other areas of my life, I could face any controversial idea or social issue without blinking an eyelash. Civil rights, gender bias, the Vietnam War, you name it, and I stood up for or against it. And, I didn't just mouth the words, I was active in the fight. But when it came to my own rights and feelings in a relationship, I turned to mush. I wavered; I defaulted; I balked.

Why was I like this? What happened to my self-confidence and courage when it came to standing up for *my* well-being? How could a strong, powerful woman like me become a jellyfish when it came to relating to men? Looking back I can see it clearly, as if looking through the rearview mirror of my car and seeing where I've been. I was very confident in helping others get what they deserved. But I didn't believe in myself or know with certainty that I also deserved what I wanted and needed. Every time I tried to stand up for myself, I knocked myself down with my own feelings of rejection. If my own father wouldn't give me the love and acceptance that I needed as a child, why should any other man? I felt completely paralyzed when it came to facing my fear of being rejected by a man I loved and needed.

And therein lies the other half of the problem. I was attracted to men who were incapable of helping me build my self-worth and overcome my childhood hurt—always the same men, just different shapes and sizes. I was constantly setting myself up for more opportunities to be rejected much in the same way my father rejected me. I got trapped in the relationship cha-chas: I would get the courage to move forward and demand the caring that I deserved only to have my partner step back and challenge my stand. The hurt little girl inside me would panic because all the feelings from childhood emerged, and any ground that I had gained turned to quicksand and sucked me down again. Eventually, I would leave the relationship, believing the next one was bound to be better. And so it was with Jake.

OTHER PEOPLE CAN'T TREAT US WITH LOVE IF WE DON'T LOVE OURSELVES FIRST

JAKE AND I didn't live happily ever after. Jake was unwilling to make a deeper commitment to our future. Like the other men in my life, he had reached the end of the line and could not give me what I needed. He could not save me from my childhood insecurities because he had his own anxieties.

At the time, my mother was dying of cancer, and I definitely needed and deserved more support from him. I was so confused and hurt. I wondered why Jake was behaving so badly at a time like this. Suddenly, the whole scene became clear to me. Jake was incapable of facing his own fear of being rejected or left behind. As Mom got closer to death, and I needed more emotional sustenance, Jake acted out his own insecurities by getting drunk and withdrawing into his own world. He left me alone to fend for myself.

It was so ironic that our relationship fell apart at this particular time. I knew the stress of a death could damage relationships, but it was much more than that. Our value systems had grown apart. I told him that I needed him to be with me, to hold me, to calm me, and to allay my fears during this horrendous experience. Day after day, I helplessly watched my mother's too-quick and painful deterioration, but Jake could only respond with coldness. This very caring man, who devoted his life to helping other people, was terrified of caring for someone on whom he depended. This may sound crazy and hypocritical, but it is all too common in many love relationships. Jake buried his feelings deeper into his work or in his beer. His actions made me feel guilty for even wanting the most basic of human care from my partner. Instead, Jake gave me an ultimatum, "Take me as I am or leave me." He said he could not give any more, and he feared that he was becoming too vulnerable.

After a terrible argument, I said to Jake: "You're always leaving when I need your help." He turned to me and said in a snide tone: "Well, what are you complaining about? You must like it because you're still here." As if struck by a thunderbolt, I suddenly sat up and took notice of what I was doing. *No, I don't like that Jake is drinking and abandoning me, and furthermore, I don't want to be a part of his abusive behavior anymore.* With complete determination and emotional calm, I looked at him and said, "You're right. I am still trying to get something from someone who has no intention of giving it. But you're wrong about my liking it. We're through." Even though Mom had lost her voice box from the cancer, as Jake walked out the door, I could hear her advice as clearly as if she were saying it to me for the first time: Demand that others treat you as well as you would treat yourself. From that illuminating moment, I learned that I had to stop being a doormat just to be loved. I had to know I counted in a relationship and wasn't with a man just to please him or satisfy his needs.

That was twenty years ago. Today, Jake is doing great.

He faced his alcohol problem and is in recovery. His dynamic passion has returned. He's back helping others and enjoying a wonderful relationship.

I don't regret one minute I spent with Jake. Through him, I learned the value of expressing myself honestly. Whenever I'm afraid of saying what I really feel, I think back to that night in Mom's kitchen, standing with the cooler in my hands, and saying, "I'll understand if you'd like to ask someone else to go camping with you, and you can still use my cooler."

WE ALL NEED LOVE AND ACCEPTANCE MORE THAN SEX!

EVEN IN OUR sex-obsessed society, it's still a fact that we human beings thrive on love, not sex. No one ever died from a lack of sex, but many have died from a broken heart.

Losing the love and respect of another person far exceeds the pang that accompanies a sexual rejection. Many of us have used sex as a substitute for love and acceptance. In spite of our auspicious, honest initial encounter, I became guilty of this in my relationship with Jake, and it proved to be dangerous. Someone can use you for sex alone and never give you any real love. You are left feeling even more unloved.

To prove the importance of love over sex, all one has to do is establish love before sex, and sexual intensity heightens a hundred times. It's much more thrilling when people who used to have sex with anyone come back and tell me how fulfilling sex is now that they're in love. And those who have to postpone or adjust their sexual expression due to illness or an accident discover the truth about love and sex—love is much more powerful.

Sex is so much more satisfying when we connect totally with someone—physically, emotionally, intellectually, and spiritually.

CHAPTER SIX

Nothing Blocks Sexual Pleasure More Than Orgasm Stress

Don't worry, you're not broken!

NOT HAVING SEXUAL PLEASURE CAUSES MORE STRESS

IT WAS 11:00 at night. The aroma of dinner's rice and vegetables and the smell of incense had filled the room. Matthew was so attentive. He had made the most delicious meal. I couldn't remember a time when a man had cooked dinner for me.

His bedroom was an extension of all that he cared about: pictures of friends and family, art posters, beads, masks, India-print cloth, and candles—so many candles around the bed. They cast a warm glow in the room and provided enough light to see each other's face and body during our lovemaking. Matthew and I had been dating each other for several months.

I met Matthew when I was working for an avant-garde theater ensemble. He was a counselor and had an office in an old church, the same place where our theater group rented space. Thank God I was working full-time and loving it. I was finally doing what I had dreamed about— working my way into a whole new lifestyle and career. It was scary but exhilarating. The theater was a lifesaver for me at a time when so much in my life was in turmoil. My mother was still battling throat cancer, and my whole family felt unsteady, as if we were living in a dark cloud. Besides the theater, I was grateful for Matthew, a wonderfully positive person who brought a smile and comfort to everyone.

Matthew would stop in to see the two founders of the theater company. We all felt better for his being there. To me he seemed a strange man because he was so content, so self-assured, and yet, so approachable. He had no protective emotional armor like most of us, no bravado, and no sarcasm. His ego was secure. Matthew was sincere; he exuded a happy energy, which was full of strength, passion, and mischief.

My five-year relationship with Jake was over, and even though I had ended it, I felt hurt, disappointed, and betrayed. At the most devastating time in my life, he had pulled away and turned his back on me. I was in such fear and pain over my mother's illness, and instead of supporting me, all Jake could do was drink for his own emotional survival.

I was so stressed and so scared. My mother's cancer was

spreading; she didn't deserve such horrible punishment. She was someone who said only nice things about others, and I was fortunate to be graced with her wisdom. She was my best friend and confidante, and I was angry that she was dying, and that she was in pain.

I watched the smoke from the incense curl around Matthew's hair and drift above the candlelight. He was massaging my legs with oil, talking ever so softly about how important it was to relax. His voice carried the same gentle touch that I felt from his hands.

Matthew massaged his way up my legs to my hips, stomach, and breasts. He treated every part of my body with sensuality and respect. He never made me feel that I had only two sexual parts: my breasts and my crotch. To Matthew the whole body was a sensual receiver, and we just needed to be tuned in to it. Making love to him was like his cooking. He knew how to carefully mix all the ingredients together so the finished creation was a culinary delight to be savored and enjoyed.

Sex was more than intercourse to Matthew. Making love with him was a very intense, fun, and emotionally satisfying experience. He was always present and totally focused. He didn't pound me during intercourse, and I felt so at ease with his slow, nonpressured approach. Every part of him moved gently and rhythmically. He communicated truthfully, and his actions matched his words. I had known so many people who said one thing but did another. Matthew checked with me at every level of our lovemaking and made sure that he never moved ahead of me. We were a team.

AN ORGASM EXPOSES US
TO OUR VULNERABILITY

AS COMFORTABLE AS I thought I felt with Matthew,
I had never actually had an orgasm with him. I felt lots of
pleasure and arousal, but never to the point of orgasm. He
did everything *right,* and I helped, too, but I had always
seemed to hit a wall or something. I chalked it up to being
with someone new, even though being with Matthew was
like being with a best friend. He didn't hide anything. He
was a giver, and I was very attracted to him.

Matthew sensed something was wrong even before I
did. It was me. Me and my stress and fears. I didn't really
understand or even recognize the problem myself.
Matthew pointed it out to me one night. We were lying
in bed at his apartment. Kyrsha was with her dad in Vermont for the weekend. Matthew asked me how my
mother was. I said, "Fine." It was my standard pat reply.
I knew my mom was in pain, but still, I quickly dismissed
his question. We started to caress and touch. I really
wanted to have an orgasm for me, for him, for us. I started
to get upset about my inability to have an orgasm because
I wanted to prove to Matthew that I worked just fine. He
never doubted it; I guess I did.

We played, rubbed, kissed, fondled, and touched each
other. Matthew was very ready, but again, he never pushed
me to satisfy himself or demand his release. He truly loved
the process as much as, if not more than, the end result.
But I was so frustrated. I was so close, and yet, I couldn't

go over the edge—the orgasm slipped away from my body like noodles off a spoon. I was so determined, and I kept trying and trying. I asked Matthew for more kissing, more touching, more rubbing, more anything. I didn't want to give up.

I felt tears well up in my eyes. I rubbed my clitoris harder and faster but it only produced more pain than pleasure. I was soaking wet; the sheets stuck to my body. I began to cry. Matthew didn't speak, instead he scooped me up in his arms and cradled me. After a few minutes, through gasps of breath, I wailed, "I don't know what's wrong with me. I don't know why I can't have an orgasm with you. It's not you. I just don't know why it won't happen."

"I think I know why," he whispered. "You're afraid to let me in. And I don't mean intercourse. You don't want to open up emotionally to me, so you can't let go of your orgasm."

What was he talking about? How did my orgasm have anything to do with my feelings for him? Besides, I felt very comfortable with him.

"It doesn't have anything to do with you, Matthew. I feel safe with you and very comfortable with you sexually."

"That's not what I mean. Having an orgasm is one way of opening up to another person. It's a very vulnerable experience. You don't want to be vulnerable with me. You're afraid. And considering what you're going through with your mother and your recent relationship with Jake, I don't blame you."

I was completely confused. How could I stop my own

orgasm? Isn't an orgasm mostly a physical reaction to sexual stimulation? I knew I needed to feel comfortable with
my partner to really enjoy our sex play, but I did feel comfortable with Matthew. He was wonderful and so attentive and caring. But what he said made some sense, and I
started to look deeper into my feelings about my mother's
illness and the leftover hurt from Jake.

For months, I felt as if I were floating in a rubber raft
that had a tiny leak; slowly and steadily, I was sinking. I
didn't even notice it, but Matthew did.

As much as I cared about Matthew and felt safe with
him, I was too afraid to really let him in. I wasn't going
to give him my orgasm because I was already so vulnerable, so exposed to pain and hurt.

Matthew was right. He was not going to get my orgasm because I needed what little protection I felt I had.
Emotionally, I was a wreck—a basket case with frayed
edges. I didn't need an orgasm. I needed to face the terror of my mother's pending death, and the sadness and disappointment from my breakup with Jake. With all the hurt
and stress inside of me, it was a wonder I could even function sexually, never mind have an orgasm. I did everything
right in terms of my sexual technique but my emotions
were unavailable. They were locked up inside me.

WE DISCONNECT FROM OUR FEELINGS IN ORDER TO FEEL SAFE

I REALIZED FROM my experience with Matthew that
most of us don't feel safe when we feel vulnerable, espe-

cially at the start of a romantic relationship. In fact, it may seem like the worst time to feel vulnerable. Even though we all long to be in love, for many of us, our worst fear is falling in love. Past experiences may have been hurtful because just as we got hooked, our partner cut the line. Then we fell back to where we were, only with a big painful hook in the mouth. So we've learned that it's better to hold back, to keep some protection up. We've learned not to expose our feelings, or to become vulnerable, or to give a partner our orgasm.

Men especially have a difficult time with vulnerability because of the way they are brought up. Little boys are taught to be strong, stifle tears, and take the pain *like a man.* We then wonder why men have such a hard time being emotional, or when they are, they are mostly angry. Men have the same emotions as women. The problem is that our society doesn't value emotional expression from men. Soldiers, policemen, athletes, super studs are not supposed to be emotional since emotional vulnerability is considered a sign of weakness. But men, like women, are human, and it is human to feel vulnerable, to feel sad, to feel any emotion.

Some of my male friends tell me that when they have intercourse with their partners, they can give their orgasm BUT cannot give their emotions. Their orgasm is merely a response to physical stimulation. They use intercourse and their orgasm to distance themselves from their partners. *I'm just going to fuck her and leave. I'm just using my dick, nothing else. I'll get off and get out before she knows the real me. I'll use my image, not my reality. It's an act. I'll boost my ego and move on to the next willing partner. If she gets hurt, it's her own fault for being so vulnerable. She can't hurt me because I don't care.*

I feel that we need to apologize to most men for the way society has duped them into believing they shouldn't feel emotionally vulnerable. I watched my father stop my five-year-old brother from kissing him good-bye because, at five, my brother was a man, and men don't kiss. Nor should they cry, or hug, or acknowledge pain or hurt. In other words, men are convinced that they shouldn't need or need to be needed. What a horrible dilemma for men! They are set up to protect their own vulnerability while they pound away at women's. I have watched many male friends and lovers keep their vulnerability packed away in their airtight hearts, and their feelings sealed off. When they do open their hearts and expose their vulnerability, the pressure is lifted, almost the way air escapes when the tab is lifted on a soda can.

When someone says to me "I don't care," what they are saying is: "I don't care to be vulnerable and risk getting hurt or rejected, so I want to be with you on my terms only. I feel much safer that way." It's too easy for men to use their sexuality as a protection against being vulnerable. When you're the one "doing it" to someone, she can't do anything to you. You're the one in control, and you're the one directing the action. At least, that's what we are brought up to believe.

Then there are some female friends who complain about the opposite. They say that the only time their male partners are emotionally vulnerable is during intercourse. They can see and feel their partner's true openness, and they relish the few moments that he is not afraid to be vulnerable. But as soon as the orgasm is over, he pulls that *safety shield* back up and rolls over.

Men are not the only ones who hide their vulnerability and emotions behind intercourse. Women have been known to experience sex without emotion. We also do it just for the physical pleasure and the ego boost. We think: *Someone, anyone, wants me tonight, at least for an hour.* We do it to hide some overwhelming pain or hurt: *I'll show you how tough I can be. You can put your dick in me, but you'll never get to my heart. No matter how hard and deep you thrust, you'll never really get close to me.*

We can all be sexual without feeling emotional, but in order to do so, we have to deliberately turn off our emotions. We have to convince ourselves to ignore our feelings and just concentrate on the physical pleasure. We justify this disconnection of our sexual expression and emotions by holding on to old myths like *That's just the way men are.* Or, *If a man can do it, so can I.* The denial grows as we continue to use sexual expression as an image booster, a status symbol, a power trip.

When we have orgasms without our emotions, or while denying our emotions, we succumb to what I call the *too-soon-to-have-sex syndrome.* We kid ourselves into thinking we are cool enough, mature enough, horny enough, or desperate enough to engage in intense sexual activity before we can even talk about it with our partner. We play with our bodies before our feelings have an opportunity to get adjusted to each other and the situation. And then we wonder why we can't let go of our orgasms. When our emotions get in the way of sexual satisfaction, as mine did, it freaks us out and makes us look at sexual intimacy in a whole new way.

Why would we want to separate any part of our being

from another? Why do we try to compartmentalize emotions, thoughts, actions, all as separate entities? We are
complex, intricately wired beings. Each part of our psy-
che pulls every other part into play. To disconnect any of
this wiring for periods of time causes a short circuit, and
in the long run, some heavy damage. If we shut down part
of us, we run on half the information. If we want to stay
balanced and better able to make positive decisions, it's im-
perative that we have all the information we need to guide
our sexuality—information about how we feel physically,
intellectually, and emotionally.

An Orgasm Is An Extension of Who We Are

THAT NIGHT WITH Matthew was the first time I rec-
ognized the important role my emotions played in my sexuality. It showed me how easy it is to pretend all is fine
and force sexual arousal. But when I did include my emotions in our lovemaking, I couldn't experience sexual pleasure.

I left Matthew that evening without having an orgasm,
but less afraid to face my mother's death, and my own pain.
Several times throughout my life, the inability to have an
orgasm had been a signal to me that there was some un-
resolved stress or fear blocking my ability to let go. My
sexuality is an expression of all of me, and my orgasms are
a true symbol of my vulnerability, my sexual self-worth,
and my feelings of love and safety with my partner. My

orgasms are one more extension of my physical, intellectual, emotional, and spiritual self.

I take care of my emotions now so that my sexuality is always connected to my feelings. And I always check my stress level before having sex. I make sure I never do anything sexually that I'm not ready for emotionally. For me, being sexual is being a physical, thinking, and feeling person. It's being the best I can be.

When I made decisions in other areas of my life, I certainly would make sure to take into consideration how I felt about what was happening, or the consequences. Yet, I would ignore my most obvious emotions when it came to sexual decisions. I wanted the best in other areas of my life: my career, the arts, as a parent, and even my recreation; so why not sex?

Orgasms are supposed to be emotion filled. That's when they feel best and give us the most positive results. I have heard over and over again from people that sexual satisfaction is a thousand times more intense and exciting when they feel loved, and feel safe with the one they love.

WE ARE ALL CAPABLE OF EXPERIENCING ORGASM

NOW THAT WE know why the best orgasms are those filled with emotion, we need to take the stress off ourselves to have orgasms as the culmination of our lovemaking. We need to realize that sex is not merely a mechanical process.

Rather it's a delicate emotional dance, and sometimes we have to communicate to our partners what's going on, as I did with Matthew.

Those of you who haven't had an orgasm yet may think that you're broken, or that you must be different from all the other easily sexually satisfied people. Well, you're not broken! Unless you have a severe injury or disability, you can experience orgasm. We all have the equipment, but we don't all give ourselves permission to feel open to sexual pleasure.

Some women get too caught up in the giving of satisfaction and are embarrassed and ashamed to accept pleasure. This attitude is emotionally damaging and hypocritical. To only care about someone else's satisfaction, and to deny your own, is really saying you are unworthy of the same love and respect.

Reaching orgasm can be very difficult when you're not proud of your body, especially your genitals. Add shame and guilt about sex that you're still carrying from childhood, and it's more than difficult—it's impossible! And, let's add a few more blocks: fear of pregnancy or a sexually transmitted disease, stress from a crisis, lack of self-worth, a selfish sex partner. You've got orgasm failure! Give yourself permission, and love yourself and your body enough to take charge of your sexual satisfaction.

Last but not least, when you cannot have an orgasm, *please don't fake it!* I am stunned when I hear sex experts tell people to fake orgasms to please a partner. A faked orgasm is dishonest, and dishonesty only leads to feelings of resentment in a relationship.

There are several reasons why we think we should fake

an orgasm: *I don't want you to think I'm not turned on. I am turned on, but I'm nervous and stressed.* Or it may be the opposite: *I don't have the courage to tell you I'm not in love with or attracted to you.* Yet another reason has more to do with fear of rejection: *If our sex life isn't satisfying to you, you might leave me.*

Our lack of sexual confidence only exposes our fears of sexual inadequacies, of being thought of as *less than* our partners. No matter the reason, being truthful is the only thing I know that brings a feeling of inner peace and gives us the strength to go through life's struggles.

DON'T EVER PRESSURE YOURSELF TO HAVE AN ORGASM

SO MANY WOMEN and men tell me how difficult it is for them to reach orgasm. For women, it's often a chronic problem; and for men, it usually starts with not getting an erection, and then later, not being able to climax. These are the very same individuals who will go for months, even years, and not say anything to their partners about their difficulty. Or they will try to cover it up with either a good fake, or just saying no to sex. All of this leads to stress, frustration, and depression. I call it orgasm stress.

We really need to understand that most women have intercourse before they ever experience orgasm, which makes having an orgasm difficult, if not impossible, to achieve through intercourse alone. Women's sexual confidence decreases as their failure rate increases.

For men, it is the opposite. They oftentimes experience orgasm as an automatic physical response that they think isn't connected to their feelings. They have so many quick and easy successes in achieving orgasm that when they face erection or orgasm failure, they are devastated, and afraid to discuss it. I have talked with many men who, at one time or another, haven't been able to reach orgasm inside their partner. They have the desire and all the physical sensation they need to achieve orgasm, but they just can't let go while they are inside their partner.

This isn't the same as worrying about getting a partner pregnant. The inability of some men to release their orgasm stems from an emotional block, not a physical problem. We make men believe that having an orgasm is all about getting pleasure, when in fact it's all about becoming vulnerable and giving a part of their total being to someone else even for a moment. Sexual expression means more than just having an orgasm. It's discovering pleasure for ourselves and our partners. It's the giving and receiving of pleasure. It's the exploration of familiar and new sexual delights. When pleasure is truly discovered and accepted, an orgasm is the by-product.

You can't force an orgasm to happen. I know, because I tried. Orgasms are supposed to help release stress, not cause more stress. And they cannot be created under great stress, as I discovered in my predicament with Matthew. So, relax! Enjoy the pleasure and the process. An orgasm is sure to come.

*I*NTERCOURSE IS THE EASIEST THING TO DO BADLY, AND THE HARDEST THING TO DO WELL

ULTIMATELY, I wish I had a dime for all the friends who have told me how unsatisfactory most of their intercourse experiences have been, and how long it took to GET IT RIGHT!

Do we pass this information on to the next generation? NO! Do we share any of our intercourse ignorance, or disappointments, with them so that they can avoid what we now know? NO! Why does this charade continue?

No one wants to admit that he or she is not really enjoying sex. No one wants to admit that intercourse doesn't bring her or him to orgasm—or that it is done with great effort, and a lot of fantasizing or pretending.

If no one has told you, let me be the first to reveal that intercourse is a very complex act that requires great trust and honesty. We must verbally communicate our needs, and do it with our eyes open.

I know couples who have been together for ten years or more and still have intercourse in the dark, with their eyes closed, without a word spoken. I don't think these couples are ready for intercourse! They need to put the lights on, open their eyes, and talk to each other.

And don't try to keep your emotions out of it! If you do, you deny yourself one of the most powerful moments of true connection with yourself and your partner.

Just having an orgasm during intercourse doesn't mean

you're even close to mastering this amazing sexual experience. No matter how long it takes to get intercourse right, it's worth it.

WE ARE AS INDIVIDUAL IN OUR SEXUAL DESIRES AND LIKES AS WE ARE IN EVERY OTHER ASPECT OF LIFE

I CONTINUALLY SAY that men and women are more similar than different, but I don't want to make it sound as if we're all exactly the same!

Individual sexual preferences are as normal and as varied as preferences in taste and talent. We all may have the same nerves and equipment, but that doesn't mean we like to use them the same way.

No two women function the same sexually, nor do any two men. This is why I resent reading books about using "the right technique" to create sexual pleasure. Someone, including myself, could rub my genitals a certain way all day, and I wouldn't necessarily get aroused. I remember when I was younger and tried the same sexual techniques that my past lover liked on a new lover, only to discover that these techniques did nothing for my new partner. You mean a penis isn't a penis isn't a penis?

To me, this is the best part about sexual individuality. It demands that we talk to our new partner and get to know him or her as a whole person, not just another collection of the same genitals. Private parts are connected to the heart, mind, and soul of an individual. They should never be lumped into "a same genital group," as if to say, *You've seen one, you've seen them all.*

Enjoy your individuality. Make sure you let your partner know that, even though we are made of the same body parts, we are not exactly like the previous partner. Erase the slate. It's time for a new lesson.

CHAPTER SEVEN

Honest Communication Builds Trust, and Trust Builds the Best Sex

How can you love me when I'm lying to you?

THERE IS NO EXCUSE FOR SUBSTANCE ABUSE

MATTHEW AND I parted as friends. I was too hurt from my breakup with Jake and paralyzed with fear over my mother's battle with cancer to give our relationship a real chance. My mother was getting very ill, and the thought of losing her made it difficult to perform even the most mundane of daily tasks.

Just before she died, I started to spend time with an old friend, Bill.

When my mother finally passed away, I was devastated. I had lost my best friend, and my grief was overwhelming. Bill was easygoing, and he seemed the perfect match for me during this time in my life. He was very laidback and had a great sense of humor. He worked for a successful landscaping company,

Bill went to work every day and helped with my theater company on weekends. I had just started my own theater company, and Bill spent many hours helping us build the sets and props. He loved Kyrsha and appeared to be a man who would be devoted to his family and would help me with my career dreams, too. We eventually moved in together.

He was a gentle lover and very willing to try new things. There wasn't any pressure from him to proceed faster than I wanted to go, and he accepted my participation in my own arousal as a good and enjoyable addition to our lovemaking. He didn't feel that he had to make me come; he just wanted to help.

Bill smoked pot, and I knew it. Unfortunately, at that time, marijuana was still considered very cool. Most of my friends also smoked pot. They didn't think it was as harmful as alcohol or other drugs. Sometimes Bill smoked at night and on the weekends, and I knew he occasionally smoked during his workday, but it didn't seem to affect him. He said it actually helped him to concentrate better on the details. But I didn't realize just how much Bill was smoking. I never questioned Bill on this issue because he was so dependable. Of course, there were those few who did nothing in life except smoke pot, but not Bill. He was ambitious and cared about his work and me.

I had tried pot when I was younger, but it didn't do a whole lot for me. I usually laughed and then fell asleep.

Mostly, I felt numb, which wasn't a feeling I liked, or silly, or totally aware of my skin or my tongue.

I loved being alert and active. Especially at this time when I was leaving my grief behind. The more I could get involved in life, the better. I was full of energy and enjoyed doing things with Kyrsha, working on my theater productions, and helping Bill with his projects. Pot would definitely slow me down, so I had no use for it. But somehow, I justified in my mind that it was okay for Bill.

Alcohol, on the other hand, was a red flag. I had dealt a lot with alcoholism during my relationship with Jake, so I was much more concerned about anyone drinking than smoking pot. My naïveté and denial soon proved me wrong.

As I started to get over the sadness from Mom's death and regain my self-confidence, I felt more energetic and wanted more out of life in general. In the beginning, Bill and I would have sex about two or three times a week. We had discovered a good routine of rubbing, kissing, mutual touching, and made sure intercourse satisfied both of us. I contributed to my own orgasm by rubbing my clitoris. We both enjoyed oral sex as an added means to our arousal or to make each other have an orgasm.

About a year after Bill and I were together, I started noticing a change in our sex life. It was a gradual change, but I remember feeling that Bill was not putting much effort into our lovemaking. Our foreplay was dwindling, and he reached orgasm much too quickly during intercourse. If I hadn't had an orgasm yet, he would touch my breasts or put his finger inside my vagina to help me climax. That was okay once in a while, but I noticed that it was happening more frequently.

He also went to work later and came home earlier. Clients began calling day and night asking for Bill, or for the estimate he was supposed to send them.

I asked Bill if he was feeling all right. I was concerned that maybe he was getting sick. I considered every reason for his behavior, from being overtired, even though he was working less, to losing interest in his job. The only thing I knew for sure was that I wasn't ready to confront him.

THE MORE YOU USE YOUR SEXUAL ENERGY, THE MORE IT WANTS TO BE USED

I WAS CONCERNED that Bill's work habits were changing, but when our sex life lost momentum, I knew we were in deep trouble. Perhaps many of you can identify with this situation. Say, for example, you haven't had any sexual contact in weeks, months, maybe even years. Some of you might not have a partner; or maybe you're not getting along with your partner; or life has become so stress filled that sex has been pushed aside. Regardless of the reason, it's a fact that sexual desire decreases with less use and increases with more use.

Too often, we believe that sexual desire is uncontrollable. I hear this from couples who have very different levels of sexual desire. I intuitively knew what was controlling Bill's sexual energy. His pot smoking was taking a toll on him. The amount Bill was smoking was truly a major problem. He was becoming withdrawn and noncommunicative. Things were tense between us.

One night we started to make love. We kissed a little and touched each other, but more and more Bill would just lie there on his back. I had to adjust my body if any movement was going to get initiated. Bill got an erection, and because I was aroused and lubricated, he rolled on top of me, and in three thrusts, he was done. I was hurt and frustrated. He apologized and offered to help me reach orgasm by fondling my breasts while I masturbated. I reluctantly agreed, but this was not what I wanted.

As I continued to masturbate, Bill rubbed my breasts with very little enthusiasm. He lacked his usual desire to participate the way he had in the past. After two or three minutes, Bill's hand started to slow down. Finally, it just stopped and was lying there on my chest like a dead weight. I looked over; he had fallen asleep. I was heartsick. I lifted his unresponsive hand off my breast and cried myself to sleep.

The next morning I was angry and confronted Bill about what had happened the night before, and, of course, he apologized. I said it was a more serious problem, and a simple apology wouldn't do. We were growing apart because of his pot smoking. I told him that I no longer believed him when he said pot didn't have a harmful effect on him. I begged him to quit, but he denied again that pot impaired him in any way. He became defensive and adamant and said with finality, "It's not a problem." I had never seen Bill so angry. He was so unwilling to take a look at my side of the picture.

Finally, I asked him to try an experiment. "If you are

so sure that marijuana doesn't affect you, then stop smoking it for three weeks and see if there's any change in your
energy level and personality." He told me it was a stupid
idea, but when I explained it was absolutely necessary for
me and our relationship he gave in reluctantly.

For three weeks Bill abstained from pot. The first
week I didn't notice much of a difference. By the second
week, Bill was a changed man. He slept less and got up
early. Projects that I couldn't get him to finish around the
house were getting his attention. We went out together
after work, and he was a ball of fire. I had never seen him
like this. He was so much more articulate. We had conversations about everything, and I was getting more than
one-word answers. He ate less and started to lose some
weight. And our sex life was back on track. He was re-
sponsive and active. Our intercourse experiences became
much more dynamic. We were loving sex partners; it was
better than when we first met.

It seemed as if I had never known the real Bill before.
He had always been stoned, and the pot had had a much
greater effect on him than I realized. I was ecstatic with
the new Bill. He was not so laid-back after all. He was
smart, witty, and more assertive. He had a very high energy level.

After the third week, I approached Bill and told him
what I had noticed. I gave him a lot of positive feedback. It
was so obvious to me that pot was depleting Bill in many
ways. I was sure that he, too, felt the difference. I was so
happy I could hardly control my enthusiasm. As I danced
around him relating all that I had witnessed, and my hope
for our continued relationship, he stood in the kitchen, leaning by the stove. He didn't say a word until I was finished.

Then he spoke. "I haven't felt any different these past few weeks. I don't know what you saw, but I was my usual self. All I felt was more uptight and anxious."

THE ONLY PERSON YOU CAN CHANGE IS YOU

I WAS SHOCKED. How could he not notice the change in himself? To some extent, he was right. He was more intense, but that's only the daily pressure we all feel as we go through life. When Bill smoked pot, he didn't feel life's natural pressures. He had numbed them out for years. Feeling them once again was overwhelming and too uncomfortable.

He was telling me that he didn't like the feeling of being "unstoned." He liked being in slow motion. He liked only doing enough to get by. He liked being in his own mind and relating on a level that suited him. He felt he had more power when he was stoned. His world was shaped by his own "stoned" perceptions. I was the one on the outside trying to get in. More afraid of living than dying, Bill went back to smoking pot. We eventually grew apart.

My experience with Bill taught me an important lesson: We cannot change our loved ones. We can only change ourselves. We can certainly be a major influence in our partner's life, but each of us has to do his or her own homework. As hard as it may seem, we have to go through our own pain, face our own fears, and take responsibility for our own mistakes.

To ANY DRUG, ALCOHOL INCLUDED, I SAY, BULLSHIT!

EACH YEAR research tells us about the bad effects of marijuana. When smoked consistently, it lowers a person's energy, alters personality, distorts reasoning, decreases ambition, lowers concentration, and numbs sexual desire. It changes our perception of time and how we relate to others.

For a very short period of time, Bill and I both tried cocaine. At first I thought it might be fun because it would give me a lift. *What the hell do I need a lift for? I already have too much energy.* The cocaine pushed me into the upper stratosphere. It was like rocket fuel; it felt dangerous. My heart pounded a lot, and I was too wired to do anything constructive. Because I was a person who liked to accomplish things, I would make lists of all the things I could do because the coke gave me more energy. I would then make another list, just in case I finished everything on the first list. All I ever accomplished on coke was making lists. The cocaine was cut with baby laxative, so mostly it "sent me" to the bathroom.

Cocaine had a worse effect on my sex drive. I was busy talking and talking about nothing, and making lists. When I tried to have sex, I was too wired to have an orgasm. Another drug myth. Coke does not increase your sex drive. Thank God, my experience with cocaine was just a short lapse of sanity. My drug experiments were over, and I was grateful that they were moderate and short-lived.

I learned a lot from Bill's dependency on marijuana

and my foolish cocaine experiment. No drug can enhance a person's sexual desire the way sexual self-esteem does. Every generation has its sex drug. Dealers try to promote its *unbelievable* effects on sexual activity. *It'll make your dick so hard for so long.* Or, *It will make your orgasm more intense.* Another, *It'll make you so horny.* Drugs are big business, and the pushers will say anything to get you hooked.

Humans are basically lazy, and we are always looking for the quick and easy solution, the drug that will "do it" for us. Nothing increases sexual desire and intensifies sexual experiences in a lasting way more than good old-fashioned, clean and sober thinking and feeling.

You may think a particular drug makes your sexual experience appear to be more intense, but in reality, it's the drug that is having the intense experience, not you.

I know what some of you might be thinking right now. *Yeah, but I've had some great sex while I was high.* That may be true, EXCEPT . . . when those sexual moments are compared to sexual experiences created with complete honesty, total awareness, and a feeling of love and respect for yourself and your partner, they are half-empty, hollow, and truly, there is no comparison.

Instead of using drugs and alcohol, we can call on the best sex tool within us—our minds. We will be higher than we can ever be on any drug when:

1. We concentrate on our own and our partner's pleasure.

2. We explore, slowly and with great care, the intensity of touching another person and ourselves.

3. We open ourselves to the positive sexual energy that flows between two caring people.

4. We give ourselves permission to enjoy our sexuality without shame or guilt.

5. We use sexual experiences to bring ourselves closer to our partner, creating more honesty and trust.

6. We add fun and laughter to one of the most intense experiences of our lives.

With time, we will reach levels that can only get more genuine and more satisfying for us. And this high never wears off because it is at our command, it is part of our beings. Self-confidence is a true high. Belief in ourselves is a true high. Instead of a drug controlling us, we direct the course of our sexual feelings, and we are in control of their intensity. And, there's no danger of overdosing!

INTERCOURSE SHOULD BE AN EQUAL-OPPORTUNITY EXPERIENCE

SOMETIMES, it takes a rude self-awakening, like the one I had with Bill, to remember that intercourse is an exchange that requires an attitude of sharing and equality. Although our lovemaking didn't start out badly, it quickly deteriorated because of Bill's drug abuse and our lack of honest, open communication. That's why I suggest to couples that they make a periodic sexual honesty check and determine that this intimate and complex sexual act brings pleasure and satisfaction to *both* partners.

To accept intercourse as an equal-opportunity experience, each partner has to believe that the other deserves equal satisfaction from the experience. The relationship is in trouble if one partner thinks he is more entitled to the experience or that his satisfaction is more important than hers.

• Both individuals have to be committed to sharing the control and be willing to give as well as receive.

• Both individuals must be willing to take charge of their own arousal and take an active part in bringing themselves to sexual satisfaction.

• Both individuals have to communicate VERBALLY (not through sign language) and never fake any orgasm or pleasure.

• Both individuals must be committed to making intercourse a physical, emotional, and spiritual connection.

And, by the way, no really satisfying sexual position is what we might think of as "romantic-looking." Let yourself go and enjoy the sensations without worrying about how you look. This a time to love, laugh, and play.

*H*ONEST COMMUNICATION BUILDS TRUST, AND TRUST BUILDS THE BEST SEX!

IF YOU LIE to your partner about sex, then it's likely that you will lie to him or her about other aspects of your partnership. In my case, I couldn't face Bill and tell him the truth until things got too miserable. Instead I cried about my orgasm because our sex life was literally going to pot.

There are many ways to lie to our partners: we say we enjoy something when we don't, or we fake an orgasm, or we say we know how to do something sexual when we've never done it before. It really doesn't matter what the lies are; it matters that we don't feel safe enough to tell the truth.

And, it isn't always our partners whom we don't trust. Lying indicates that we don't feel too good about ourselves. At first, I didn't believe I was lovable or desirable to Bill. I didn't believe that the real me was good enough, and I didn't trust that I had the right to be satisfied or the right to confront him. So, the lies continued, and I grew more and more frustrated and resentful of a dissatisfying sexual situation.

And what's worse, it's difficult to believe in your partner once you begin lying. I would wonder, *How can you love me when I'm lying to you?* Love lies erode trust between two people and eventually cause a relationship to deteriorate.

Telling the sexual truth makes it easier to be truthful

in other areas of the relationship. Once you're able to honestly communicate who you are sexually, it's so much easier to be honest about how you really feel and what you need. Here is a sample of one of my actual love lie confessions:

> *I need to tell you something that is difficult for me to say. First, I want you to know I do truly love you and want you to trust me. The only way you will learn to trust me is if I tell you the truth. I also want our sex life to keep getting better, so by my telling you this, I am also proving to you that I am committed to being the best lover I can. I have been unhappy with the quality of our intercourse, and I apologize for not expressing this sooner. I was afraid you would think that it was all your fault or that I wasn't turned on by you. This is not the case. I am still very turned on by us. I need to let you know what I like and desire. I have been too passive, and I have been letting you take total control. I feel that you need to be aggressive in order to get sexually aroused, so I literally lie back and let you take over. This isn't fair to you or me. I want to build a sex life that is satisfying to both of us and is based on the giving and receiving of real pleasure. So I hope you accept my apology for not telling you sooner, and I hope you will let me show you more of what works for me and help me find new sexual pleasures.*

My partner's reaction was a hug, and this response:

> *I really appreciate your telling me this. I do have trouble with control. I have always tried too hard or felt ob-*

ligated to please my partner. Sometimes, it was a way
to keep myself from becoming emotionally vulnerable, so
I wouldn't get hurt. If I took the sexual control, then I
felt safer. I now realize that I didn't let in my emotions.
I want to let you in. I am vulnerable to you, and I do
feel safe. I'm sorry, too. I'll try to be less controlling dur-
ing intercourse.

Then he said the best thing: "It will take us at least a year
to get this intercourse thing right." We both laughed and
marked the calendar.

Lasting trust only comes from being honest. Sometimes
we think we trust someone before we really know the person, but that isn't real trust. Rather, it is the desire to trust.
The trouble is that desiring to trust is not the same as real
trust. It is an illusion we have created in order to try to get
the love we so desperately need. The key word here is *desperately*. Desperation doesn't help to nurture honesty or
trust. Desperation leads us down all kinds of false roads of
love. Ultimately we feel worthless and hopeless. Being
honest with myself helped me to trust myself more and
lessen my desperate need for love and acceptance.

Trust based on honesty means feeling and knowing we
are in a safe sexual place: safe enough to explore; safe
enough to be vulnerable; and safe enough to participate
in a relationship on all levels—physically, emotionally, intellectually, and spiritually.

A little while back I mentioned the idea of sexual
amnesty. Most of us get ourselves deep into resentments
before we even openly admit that there is a problem. For
so many reasons, we are masters of avoiding small issues
until they grow into major problems. Sexuality is a major

issue in a relationship. Our sex life is in many ways a reflection of our whole relationship. It can be good and bad, painful and joyful, a failure or a success. And if our sexual transgressions aren't too many or too devastating, most of our resentments and sexual issues can be fixed.

The first step is giving each other sexual amnesty. Amnesty provides the freedom for us to continue to build a mutually satisfying sex life. It permits us to become more concerned with the solution than with who is to blame for the problem. We can't fix the partnership unless both partners help with the solution. It is hard to be part of the solution if you are always criticized as being the problem.

The next step involves forgiving ourselves and forgiving our partners. It is the quickest way to a new beginning. Resentment builds walls to keep out further disappointments and hurt. But these walls also keep out love. Walls may feel necessary to protect us, but they only create more isolation and loneliness.

If you are stuck in a sexual rut and honest communication has broken down, here are some truth-telling tips:

1. Forgive yourself so it is easier to admit the truth. Don't beat yourself up.

2. There is no guarantee that your partner will be as forgiving. Tell the truth for yourself because it is the right thing to do. Many times partners can forgive when a sincere apology is given. The key word here is *sincere*.

3. Use words and a tone of voice that are not defensive. How we tell the truth is important, too.

It shows our willingness to take responsibility for our dishonesty.

4. Don't "tell the truth" and in the same sentence blame your partner for your lie. It's a fact that many partners don't make it easy to tell the truth. Remember, the lie was our choice as a means of dealing with the situation to begin with.

5. Get all the truth out the first time. If we are asking our partners to trust us, don't sabotage the process by holding back part of the lie. It will only surface at a later time.

Telling the truth takes time and practice. Be patient with yourself and your partner. Most of us were not brought up to feel comfortable discussing our sexual needs in an honest way. And try not to take the truth so personally that you are incapable of putting it into perspective and moving forward. I assume you bought this book because you know you deserve the best love and the best sex. Don't throw it all away because of past resentment and hurts.

BE HONEST ABOUT YOUR SEXUALITY

BECAUSE I WASN'T getting what I needed sexually from Bill, I had to speak up for myself and my needs. At first I was angry, which gave me the courage to ask him to change his behavior. Then, I had to examine how honest I was being with myself and my sexual desires. I certainly didn't want a partner falling asleep in the midst of our lovemaking, or coming to orgasm long before my own arousal.

The best thing about being honest about my sexuality was that I really learned about my own pleasure needs. I learned what I needed to be satisfied, and what brought me to orgasm. I started to accept my sexual self.

Being honest with yourself encourages you to explore and grow without pressure or fear of failure. And when you are being true to yourself and your partner, you gain the confidence to continue to express yourself honestly.

Today, I can say the words that describe who I am sexually and what I am striving for in the future. In fact, being able to describe who you are sexually is a great exercise in becoming more honest with yourself. I'll go first, then you try:

I am very sexual, but I need to have my sexual experiences, especially intercourse, connected to all the other parts of me—my emotional and spiritual sides. I have tried being sexual only in a physical way, and I can go through the motions, maybe even have an orgasm, but why would I want to? I feel more empty than full, more confused than confident, as well as disconnected from my total self.

I can only feel sexually uninhibited when I feel emotionally safe.

I like and need to help myself have an orgasm. I don't have orgasms merely through vaginal stimulation. I need to rub my clitoris at the same time. I have had orgasms during intercourse when on top, but a lot of times, it requires too much unnecessary work.

I don't have orgasms through oral sex yet, but I'm working on it. If I do, fine, but I won't feel bad if it never happens. It still gets me very excited. I love having my partner use his finger in my vagina, too.

I have a difficult time having an orgasm when I'm overtired or stressed. Orgasms help me to relax.

I love to laugh during sex play. I like watching ourselves in the mirror. I like to have enough light to see what we're doing.

My breasts and nipples are very sensitive, and I love to have them caressed. And having my neck kissed makes me shiver.

I like starting intercourse very slowly. The slower we go, the faster I reach orgasm.

So, that's a lot about who I am sexually, right now. I know I will continue to grow and change. It's your turn.

A TRUE HIGH COMES FROM FEELING OUR OWN WORTH

SEXUALITY IS ABOUT connecting the physical with our emotional and spiritual selves. It's only through looking inward and unraveling our complicated sexual fears and beliefs that we become more aware. Discovering these fears and beliefs may take some time, but the results are tangible. As you become more aware, you will learn the definition of being in a higher state. No drug can do this. Only your own mind and will can. Looking outside yourself for a sexual high only becomes a contradiction.

Bill and I did not have an honest relationship, sexual

or otherwise. It was built around his drug use, and my acceptance of that use. I was too insecure to face his dependency on drugs, and he was too caught up in a cloud of smoke to see the truth. *No relationship can last when drugs or alcohol are involved.* No drug can truly enhance sex, which should be experienced with all our natural senses, feelings, and spiritual energy. Furthermore, we really can't communicate honestly and openly while on drugs or alcohol. These substances only build a wall between two people and cause a loss of trust in the relationship.

We need to be truthful with those of our own generation and with generations to come. I have never been as *high* as I am today. Why? Because I have never felt so loved and so confident in my own self-worth. I'm not talking about career success or *making it* in the outer, material world. It's about my own personal growth. I no longer make excuses, or need to create artificial detours, or put up roadblocks in my life. I have made solid and steady progress, one step at a time. I can depend upon myself. I have learned to reach into the deepest parts of myself to tap real courage, strength, and self-reliance. The only hangover is self-esteem. I wake up knowing that there is always more to be gained, more to learn, more to feel, and more work to be done. And so much more to appreciate.

No drug can do all that.

Word of mouth is the greatest promoter of drug use. Wouldn't it be more beneficial to tell the truth to one another—that clean and sober sex is the greater high? Spread the word.

CHAPTER EIGHT

Taking Charge of Your Sex Life

It's all about thinking before you have sex.

ANOTHER SEXUALLY TRANSMITTED DISEASE RAGES ON

AROUND 1981, I started to read about an illness that was striking young gay men. No one knew the cause of this new disease, and anyone who had it died a quick, quiet death. An alarm went off inside me: I didn't want such a horrible thing to happen to my brother, Jimmy.

Jimmy was gay but not effeminate. In fact, he hated effeminate men. Okay, he didn't hate them; he just wasn't attracted to them. I often told him, "You're a macho chauvinist," and both of us would laugh. I was very proud

of my "little" brother. Like my "big" sister, he battled an
alcohol addiction and won. He then dared to move away
from our small town with its homophobic mentality.

The only way I could learn about this sickness was
through gay newspapers that Jimmy brought home, or
from some small article hidden on the back page of the
Boston Globe. The medical community was panicked, yet
there were no comments to the public about the severity
of this new disease called AIDS. I wanted to get involved
in this quiet epidemic because it was personal to me. After
all, my brother was gay, and this illness seemed to target
gay men. Since I had been a drug-hotline volunteer back
in the late sixties, I knew I had the ability to help somehow. So, I called the only organization in Massachusetts
that was providing care and education for people with
AIDS, and I became a volunteer.

I began my AIDS work and safer-sex odyssey in the
cellar office of the AIDS Action Committee in the heart
of Boston. At the time, all I knew was that a virus was
transmitted through sex, blood transfusions, and intra-
venous drug use. For many, sex was the most probable
route of transmission. What I didn't know was that my
work with people with AIDS would help me to discover
that *safe sex* was not necessarily about preventing a disease.

So there we were, the best-educated volunteers for
one of the first AIDS organizations in the country. Community associations demanded AIDS information, and we
scrambled to get the word out. We knew more about the
virus and its ensuing illness than most, and we became a
small, knowledgeable band of volunteers ready to fight
against the spread of this epidemic. We went into the
community to try to recruit everyone, gay and straight, to

join our cause. We knew all too well not only that we were at risk of losing someone we loved, but also that we might become infected ourselves.

Heartbreaking as it was, young gay men were dying of AIDS, and they were dying alone. Not only did they hide their lifestyle from their parents, but with the onset of AIDS, these young men faced their worst nightmare. They had to tell their parents that they were gay, and that they had a disease that would surely take their lives. Most hoped their families would help them in such dire need; and, thankfully, some did. Unfortunately, many didn't. As an AIDS volunteer and trained hospice worker, I was among many brave people who helped these young men to face their fear, and in many cases, to face their death, hoping for a more accepting and loving afterlife. I learned that we had to share love instead of fear.

THE FACTS ABOUT SEXUALLY TRANSMITTED DISEASE

HERE'S WHAT I learned about sexually transmitted diseases, or STDs: You can catch HIV (the AIDS virus), syphilis, gonorrhea, venereal warts, chlamydia, and the whole gang of microorganisms and parasites from a single sexual encounter, or you can luck out, have sex with a bus-load of strangers, and not catch anything at all. At this point, I need to state the obvious: the more sexual partners you have, the greater your risk of taking home something you don't want.

Our immune system is our body's defense network,

and its job is to destroy or neutralize foreign substances like someone else's semen or vaginal fluid. Repeated invasions can leave it weakened. We weren't designed to overload our systems with a variety of bacteria-filled fluids. Our immune system has only so much fight in it. Excessive stress can also reduce its ability to defend our bodies. Drugs, including alcohol and tobacco, cause even more damage to the immune system. Poor nutrition takes its toll, and pollutants kill off the rest of our immune cells. Doctors and scientists tell us that a weakened immune system increases our chances of contracting a virus that, once introduced into our bodies, can grow and multiply rapidly.

Over time, many cures for STDs have been discovered, and with each new antidote, we are reprieved once again from the risk of infection. As soon as we feel safe and free again, WHAM! We're hit with a new disease that is stronger than any antibiotic. And today, that disease is known as AIDS.

A CONDOM IS OUR HOTLINE TO SAFER SEX

DURING BREAKS AT our AIDS education meetings, Eric, a very funny and loving gay male educator, and I would "dish the dirt" about the new loves in our lives. Like relationship cheerleaders, we gave each other encouragement and support for success in love.

I had been dating a guy named Bob for a few months, and I really liked him. I was hoping that he wanted to try to build a committed relationship, but it was too early to tell. Bob and I talked about so much—our past, our present, and our future goals. Like every new couple, we put our best selves forward and, so far, the relationship was developing nicely.

Eric, too, had a new love in his life, and both of us admitted that we were going to "do it" with our partners. We had waited what we thought had been a really long time, working slowly up to this special event. Eric and I were well informed about risky sexual activities, and we practiced with each other how we planned to talk with our partners about safer sex. We knew, more than most, how important it was to use a condom. We also knew, better than most, how to use one correctly. No one was more prepared for practicing safer sex than Eric and I. We knew that if people could accept that certain ways of having sex will *always* be risky, then they would be less likely to fall into the trap of false security.

We also knew that the main reason why many of us keep getting into trouble is that we are using our genitalia all wrong. Here's how:

Anal Intercourse (a penis in a rear end) has always been risky because of the way the anus is constructed, no matter if you're a man or a woman. The thin tissue inside the anus tears easily. Even a nutshell that is eaten by mistake and passes through the anal passage can tear this delicate tissue. It doesn't open wide, and it doesn't stretch, either. So putting a big, hard penis in the anus can tear it. Fingernails are dangerous, too. Anything used too vigorously can cause rips and abrasions.

If there's a tear in the walls of the anus (even a microscopic one), bacteria, germs, and viruses (including HIV) can be deposited directly from a penis into the blood system. Even if there are no tears, some germs still can pass through the tissue and cause infection. Even dirt from fingernails causes infection. HIV doesn't make putting a penis in a rear end risky. It has always been a risky sexual activity.

Vaginal Intercourse has its risks, too. Granted, the vagina is designed to accommodate a penis because it is stronger and more flexible than the anal passage. The tissue inside the vagina is more resilient, and it can take some thrusting, prodding, and friction without being damaged. But it is not indestructible. Thrusting too hard and too long can cause irritations on the inner and back walls of the vagina, allowing germs, bacteria and viruses to enter the bloodstream. The opening at the back of the vagina, the cervix, allows sperm and germs to enter the bloodstream through the uterus. Pounding a penis in and out of the vagina can push against the urethra, forcing germs into a woman's bladder, which causes urinary infections. And, of course, there is always the risk of pregnancy.

Men aren't out of the woods either. When a penis gets irritated from too much dry friction, germs can enter the blood system through small sores. The end of the penis has a hole that opens into two tubes, one for urine and one for semen. These tubes are made of delicate tissue that can also become damaged or irritated during vaginal intercourse.

Finally, let's look at **Oral Sex,** which means putting a penis in the mouth, or putting a mouth on a vulva, or putting a tongue into a vagina or anus. If a guy has a sexually transmitted bacteria or virus on his penis, it can be transmitted into the mouth. Some germs on the penis skin or in the preorgasm fluids, as well as semen, are capable of going through the membranes of the mouth and getting into the blood system. And, if the penis rubs too hard and long in the mouth, it can cause sores inside the mouth. The same thing occurs when a mouth comes in contact with a vulva and vagina. Vaginal fluid, like semen, can carry viruses like HIV. There is also an added factor: Women can have blood (usually small amounts) in their vaginas even when they are not having their periods. It may be a harmless amount, but it does pose an added risk to the person performing oral sex.

Finally, when oral sex involves the rear end, germs too numerous to count are introduced into the body via the mouth. Parasites that live in feces, if swallowed, can colonize in the digestive tract, causing pain, diarrhea, and other problems that are difficult to cure.

So here they are. The facts that have been ignored far too long.

TEENS AND SEX. YES, THEY DO IT!

BECAUSE I WAS the only AIDS educator with a preteen daughter, I was drafted to speak about safer sex at our local high schools. As a straight woman, I was more acceptable to most PTAs and school boards. At my first lecture, I captivated 1,500 teenagers. Even the teachers were enthusiastic. It was a major event in my life as well as theirs. Those teens and I talked openly and explicitly about sexual activities. I was sure that most teachers didn't know such sexual practices existed among their students. I felt good about my ability to help educate this very vulnerable generation.

Adults often think that teens believe they're immortal. I don't remember feeling superhuman between the ages of twelve and twenty. I felt insecure. I fretted, obsessed, and cried about something every day. I worried a lot about death. I felt more pessimistic and fatalistic than at any other time in my life. I believed that I was a magnet for bad shit. Yet, I still took risks: I drove fast, drank too much, tried drugs, shoplifted, cheated, lied, broke rules, and ignored curfews. My need to try new things was much stronger than my fear of punishment. I knew I might get into trouble, big trouble, but I thought I would be in bigger trouble emotionally if I didn't go after what I thought I needed. Most of all, I feared everything.

I couldn't share many of my feelings. I knew that the world didn't like teenagers. We were irresponsible pains in the ass and adults couldn't relate to us. We resented our low status and made conscious efforts to do exactly what they expected teens to do. Like almost every other kid, I knew when adults were exaggerating about something. They wanted to scare us out of doing things. We knew this tired old trick. It insulted our intelligence, and we became more anxious to rebel.

Unfortunately, adults still use the same tactics—hell and damnation, and the threat of death. But threats don't work. In fact, statistics say our chances of getting an STD are greater than ever, yet each generation starts having intercourse at a younger age. We need to start telling our kids the whole truth about sex and not think we can outsmart them through fear tactics.

WHY IS IT SO DIFFICULT TO ASK OUR PARTNERS TO WEAR CONDOMS?

THREE NIGHTS AFTER my first teen sex talk, I found myself entangled in my boyfriend's arms and legs. *Okay, Suzi, now is the time to bring out the condom,* I said to myself. It was in the drawer next to the bed. It was only inches from my fingers. Bob was lying on top of me, and I felt his erection between my thighs ready to slide into my vagina.

I thought to myself: *Let go of his shoulder and reach down and pick up that condom and say, "Let me help you put this on." He won't mind; he's so considerate of my feelings and needs. Yeah, but he might think that I have a sexually transmitted disease, or worse, that I think he has one! Well, he might; that's why we need to use a condom. He told me that he hadn't been with many people, so the chances of his having HIV is remote, almost impossible. Why am I going to risk upsetting him? He's so excited, and if we stop now, he might lose his erection and get really embarrassed.* I decided that it was okay not to use a condom this time, but if it was anyone else, I would definitely have the guy put one on.

I blew it. I talked myself out of using a condom, and all the excuses came from me! I didn't even ask him! A few days ago, I had said to an auditoriumful of teenagers, "Wait to have intercourse. If you're not going to wait, *use a condom!*" I knew that if they couldn't use a condom, they weren't ready for intercourse. So what about me? How could I be so dumb? What happened to all my training and experience? Even with the threat of HIV, I couldn't ask my partner to put on a condom.

The fact is, not enough people use condoms.

This surprised some experts, but certainly not me. Sex educators thought that AIDS statistics would make people rush to pharmacies where they'd load up shopping baskets with rubbers. But when it didn't happen, celebrities were asked to speak out about HIV to drive up condom sales. Even that didn't help.

The truth is, more people will start using condoms when their attitudes change. Up to now, every ad that uses sex to sell a product perpetuates the notion that great sex, specifically intercourse, is wordless and spontaneous. It's about time that advertisers start selling sex images that include the use of condoms and support the postponement of intercourse. I'd like to see condoms promoted as readily as seat belts and beer. We have few moral qualms about advertising alcohol, which kills and destroys more lives and families than all other drugs put together, but we cannot advertise a vital health device like a condom. Fortunately, we now have an administration in Washington that promotes condom use through public service announcements on TV, but ordinary commercials for condoms are still sporadically aired.

Campaigns that promote condom use, for the most part, have been directed at men. But men continue to resist using condoms, so the newest attempt has been to get women to demand that their partners use them. But like me, before women can demand condom use each and every time, they have to feel the strength that comes from their own self-worth and dignity. As long as women believe that sex means more to men than to themselves, they will remain silent, and men who don't feel like using condoms will get their way.

Why didn't I do what I was trained to help others to do? What part of my system broke down? What happened in that bed that I wasn't prepared for? I was so shaken by this failure that I almost didn't go to my next volunteer meeting. How could I tell Eric? I thought, *No more AIDS education lectures for you, Suzi.*

At first break, Eric asked me about my night with "Mr. Wonderful." I waited a moment before I answered; then I blurted out the truth. "I didn't use a condom. In fact, I didn't even bring up the subject." I felt so ashamed. Eric didn't answer me. I knew I had disappointed him. Suddenly, he leaned in very close and put his arm around my shoulder. He whispered, "I didn't either."

I thought to myself, *What's going on?* How could we fail at changing our sexual behavior when we were the so-called experts? We had education, training, and experience. It was obvious that we both had more to learn.

DESPERATE NEEDS ARE ALWAYS MORE POWERFUL THAN WELL-BEING NEEDS

MY WORK WITH people with AIDS triggered a greater shift in my sexual attitudes. I began to examine more deeply the reasons behind our sexual encounters and why self-worth and sex go hand-in-hand. I learned from my own behavior that the threat of catching a sexually transmitted disease, even AIDS, is not enough to change our sexual behavior.

The AIDS epidemic is on the rise, yet researchers say that in some groups the percentage of people using condoms has increased only slightly. Again, I'm not surprised. Fear of pregnancy does nothing to reduce the incidence of vaginal intercourse.

If we were strictly rational beings, the threat of a potentially lethal virus that is transmitted to our bodies during anal, vaginal, or oral sex would deter us from playing this type of sexual Russian Roulette. But sexual expression is not based on rational thinking. If we fear rejection, loneliness, physical and/or emotional abuse more than we fear infection, then we are willing to cock the trigger, point, and squeeze. If we take a risk and don't catch anything, the experience can induce a feeling of relief and power. Beating the odds fools us into believing that the risk is an exaggeration. "I've had a lot of sexual experiences, and I never caught an STD," some say. When risky sex is connected to AIDS, those who are lucky can pretend that those who aren't must have done something wrong. A series of empty chambers gives us a sense of false confidence, and we continue playing the game.

My failure to use a condom was the start of a great personal triumph. I thought about this incident for weeks, even months, before I could figure it out. First, I took a hard look at myself. Even though my feelings of self-worth had increased over the years, I was still very insecure in relationships. My greatest fear was having someone I needed reject me. I was desperate for acceptance and validation, especially from a male partner. This one fear could,

and did, overpower any courage or strength I had accu-
mulated from other aspects of my life. I had stood my
ground in some of the most hostile situations—at my
job, or in my community, or when protecting someone I
loved. In those instances, I would stand up for myself and
defend others. However, when it came to my partner's
love, my behavior was coming from pure desperation.

All the little-girl hurt caused by my father's emotional
abuse and rejection was still running my life. It replaced
all the greatest of intentions and any common sense I may
have had. My safer-sex education wasn't as important to
my self-esteem as my emotional needs were. Or so I believed at the time. The balance between what I knew was
right and what I needed emotionally was lacking. I needed
Bob to want me more than I needed to do the right thing
and protect my life from AIDS.

I knew in my heart that I couldn't guarantee success
or change my sexual behavior if I didn't first fix my need
for acceptance and approval. Crazy as it seemed, *I was willing to die just to be loved.* This desperate need to be loved
scared me even more than the AIDS virus. I finally understood why men and women took such monumental
risks with their lives to be with someone they thought they
needed, because I felt the same way.

As much as sociological and psychological research tell
us that a human being's strongest drive is to stay alive,
many of us continue to choose emotional well-being over
physical survival. Researchers don't take into consideration our emotional behavior. They underestimate the pain
of loneliness and the desperate desire to be needed and
loved, even for one superficial moment.

I knew that I was destined to repeat my failure in the

bedroom with another "Mr. Wonderful" if I didn't change my lack of self-worth and self-love. I knew that *safe sex* had to do with feeling safe with my partner, enough to tell him the truth. I also knew that sexual information and education could not make me change old patterns of behavior. After all, I relied on those patterns for many years; they helped to ease my fear of being rejected. As a child, I tried so hard to get my father to love me. As an adult, I often put myself in harm's way for one mere moment of validation from someone else.

The fear of rejection can make us do loony things. A lot of us decide to have a sexual encounter with someone, even though we might not want to. But we desperately need an encounter, any encounter. Almost unconsciously, we find ourselves performing the sex act. We pretend our way through it, even telling ourselves that it's great. We try to fill emotional needs by sexually acting out. Used this way, sex doesn't fill those needs. Instead it leaves us empty, hurt, confused, angry, and sometimes infected.

I didn't realize that to feel safe, I had to believe in myself. I had always looked to my relationships with others to make me feel important. If they liked me, I was okay. I did more than my share of making the relationship work. But if I wasn't getting what I needed, I felt resentful. I tried so hard to please the other person, and I put up with so much bullshit. Instead of counting on myself to feel good, I counted on others. I didn't want to face the fact that my partner had no intention of creating a mutually happy and satisfying relationship. After all, he had his own emotional demons to face, too. So, when one relationship ended, I moved quickly to the next. I didn't want to feel that terrifying emotional void in my gut. It hurt too much. It re-

minded me of the times when I was little and I felt so
unimportant.

I understood the psychology of human behavior, especially mine, yet I only knew it in my head. And, I certainly was tired of feeling like a failure. But how could I
do what I knew was right to do?

Now came the really tough homework. I had to be
the doctor and pay a house call on myself to make a personal inner examination. This one would pain me more
than any MD's probing and prodding.

- I was finished with saying one thing and doing
  another.

- I was through being a hypocritical "know-it-
  all."

- I could no longer be an altruistic volunteer and
  not practice what I preached.

THE BIGGEST SEXUAL SELF-CONFIDENCE BATTLE IS ALWAYS FOUGHT AND WON WITHIN YOURSELF

IT WAS TIME to face myself and confront my self-
sabotaging fears. I realized that I needed to renew my
committment to build my sexual self-confidence.

I love the term *sexual self-confidence*. And it's important
to put the word *sexual* before *self-confidence*. I say this be-

cause I have met many people who are self-confident in
several areas of their lives except their sexuality. I have noticed, too, that when we are self-confident in other areas
of our lives, it doesn't necessarily transfer to our sexuality.
On the other hand, when we become truly sexually self-
confident, it always affects other parts of our lives. This happens, I believe, because our sex lives are the most complex
parts of our beings, and solving issues here helps to solve
other issues. When we take charge of our sexual attitudes
and behavior, we're cleaning out and organizing our sexual closet, and we take charge of our lives in general.

Sexual self-confidence means replacing shame and fear
with a strength of conviction. This new conviction lets us
know that we are valuable, and our sexual choices help to
support our well-being and the well-being of our partners.
In other words, we believe in ourselves and accept our sexuality; we integrate our sexual experiences into our total
physical, emotional, and spiritual health. Sexual self-
confidence is an important part of loving ourselves and
loving our partners.

The first thing I had to do in my sexual recovery program for safer sex was to be brutally honest with myself in
my day-to-day living. I had to make a commitment to myself that I would not lie about anything, especially my sex
life. If I could be honest with myself about something as
scary or judgmental as sex, then it might be easier to tell
the truth about most other things. Actually, I found this
to be true.

Second, I pledged to take one day at a time. I couldn't
trust my emotional needs because they could seduce and
manipulate me. I knew that my emotions had forced me
to make unwise choices in the past. I didn't have to worry

about others hurting me; I was doing a great job all by my-self.

In order to believe I was valuable and deserved the best care, I had to treat myself well:

• I had to stand up for myself and care for me before I could truly care for others.

• I had to believe that it was *not okay* to sacrifice myself for another's needs. This was simply low self-esteem.

• I had to believe that as a woman I was equal in value to men. To accept a lesser ideal was destructive to myself and my relationships.

• I could never let my sexual expression put myself, or my partner, at risk—physically, emotionally, or spiritually.

• I had to believe that telling the truth is the only way to build true self-worth and self-respect.

These attitude changes made the greatest difference in my behavior, especially my sexual behavior. I now had some clear and specific beliefs that could guide me when I had to make tough personal decisions:

• I didn't feel the need to have intercourse because *he wanted it*. Intercourse was no longer a substitute for self-acceptance.

• I didn't have to pretend to be sexually satisfied to make someone else feel good. What's the point in that, anyway?

• I didn't have to be someone's sex object. I wasn't *something to play with.*

• I didn't have to use sex to feel needed or important.

ALWAYS THINK ABOUT SEX BEFORE YOU DO IT!

WE KNOW NOW that thinking about sex before we do it is not exactly a popular idea. When I say *think about it,* I mean more than just thoughts. For instance, I was talking to a young man the other night. At thirty-two, he had only been with women, and he had just had his first sexual experience with another man. It was also an anonymous sexual encounter, and he was concerned about contracting AIDS.

I was more concerned about how he felt about the experience. When I asked, "Why did you do it?," his reply was, "It was a spur-of-the-moment kind of thing." WAIT A MINUTE! Having oral sex for the first time with someone of the same gender was just a spur-of-the-moment kind of thing?!? I didn't buy it, so I pressed him further. Sure enough, he had thought about it for a long time but never talked to anyone about his desire. By not talking about it, he didn't have the knowledge to be cautious. He never asked himself: (1) why he desired this type of sex; (2) where the desire came from; (3) why he acted it out at this particular time; and (4) why it occurred under anonymous circumstances? He had only thought about the act itself, not his feelings about it. He never questioned himself, so in essence, *he never really thought about it.*

I told him the next time he wanted sex, he had to ask all the really hard questions, and then talk to someone who wouldn't judge but could help him understand the *whys* not just the *hows*.

Sexuality isn't about an act; it's about beliefs. By uncovering the source of my fears, I had figured out what was driving my actions. I just couldn't improve my sexual performance and be done with it; I had to improve my sexual attitudes.

Before my attitude change, I was driving my sexuality as if I were driving a car that had shoddy brakes and no steering wheel. By valuing the emotional, physical, and spiritual aspects of my sexual well-being, I became a confident driver. I was ready to handle the various road conditions of life's AAA trip ticket. I knew I could still veer off onto some rocky trails but would always return to the main road for an attitude adjustment. I figured out that when I make a wrong turn, it's connected to a bad attitude that snuck in when I wasn't paying attention to the road ahead.

CHAPTER NINE

Learning from Our Relationship Mistakes

Don't beat yourself up!

No MATTER HOW STRONG I BECAME, I STILL FELT LIKE THE WEAKER SEX

My friend Parker, who grew up in South Carolina, had a unique slang for saying we can eventually learn or change. Parker's version was a bit more colorful. He would say, "You don't have to slap me in the face with a fish all day, I wake up about noon!" In other words, *Eventually, I get it*.

For me, my *noon* was quickly approaching. I was sexually self-confident, more than I had ever been, yet I was still feeling unsteady. I was determined to make a relationship *happen* for me, and I believed in trying until I got it right. I guess you can say I had admirable determination, but I was trying to make something happen *before* I had all the tools. It was like trying to build a house with only a hammer and a screwdriver. The end result was a house that was still under construction and too rickety for habitation.

Fortunately, I was growing in confidence through the nourishment I received from my AIDS and safer-sex education work. It was 1986, and I was using my performing talents to inspire others to change their attitudes about their sex lives and their relationships. I was learning while teaching. Sometimes I was way ahead of my students, and other times I was merely a few steps further along the road to self-worth. I was eager to apply my newly formed attitudes to my own relationships. I ran onto the dating field like so many players filled with potential, but, like an athlete recovering from an injury, I was going back into the game too soon.

During this period, I got interested in bodybuilding and started to work out at a gym every day. It was a place that helped me to develop emotionally as well as gain physical strength. My weight training became a symbol for my emotional healing, and I wanted to get stronger and healthier in every way. Gradually, I advanced to heavier weights and a more intense workout. I broke my training into sections, concentrating on one part of my body at a time. I learned the correct form to get the most out of my exercise routine, and I enjoyed my newly acquired sense of self-discipline. I was accomplishing what I set out to do, and I was getting stronger and healthier.

Eventually, I joined a new gym in order to train on

better equipment and with people who were a bit more serious than those at the local health spas and fitness centers. After two months, I had not really talked with anyone. I liked working out alone because I could concentrate on what I was doing to gain more strength and power. It was exciting for me. As a woman, I had never really felt physically strong, not like the men I knew. No one had ever encouraged me to discover my inner strength or physical power. Yes, I played sports, took dancing lessons, and trained as a gymnast, but I always felt limited. I was taught that most women were not physically strong, or that we did not have the ability to develop an impressive amount of muscle. Even if we could overcome the first two obstacles, we certainly couldn't stick to a hard training routine.

In the gym, these types of messages were sent out *loud and clear*. When women came upstairs to use the free-weight equipment, I could hear the men grumble to themselves, "Why don't they stay downstairs on the machines. They're interrupting my workout." Yet, when these same men trained together, pressing steel bars loaded with iron plates, they had no trouble motivating one another. "Don't be a PUSSY! Press it, you WUSS! You lift like a girl!" These same men who dubbed each other "pussy" as a form of negative name-calling spent most of their waking hours preening and pumping just to find some of the same. I didn't care if I interrupted their workouts, because mine was just as important to me. I kept to myself and felt prouder than ever of my femininity.

One evening, I decided to try to bench-press more than my usual weight and psyched myself for the challenge. I lay back on the bench, placed my hands on the bar, took a deep breath, and lifted the bar off the rack. Slowly, I brought the bar to my chest for the big blast up. I pressed with all my strength, and I struggled to lift the bar. It moved slowly, inch by inch. I closed my eyes and squeezed my facial muscles hoping these gestures would help me get the bar back on its rack. While my eyes were closed, I heard, "Come on, you can do it! Come on, keep pushing." I opened my eyes and there was a man with a mustache and long hair hanging over me. I saw his hands go under the bar in case my arms and chest weren't strong enough to bring it back home. I pushed with every fiber of muscle in me to reach the rungs. *I did it!* I felt his hands quickly pull back the bar and lock it safely on its stand.

He looked at me sincerely. "You work harder than any of the guys in here."

I said, "Thanks," and asked his name.

"Tony," he replied, smiling. He was built big but not as big as the professional bodybuilders. We talked for a few minutes about weight training and then awkwardly returned to our separate routines.

FEAR OF LONELINESS LED ME TO ANOTHER DISCONNECTED RELATIONSHIP

WITH ALL MY newly developed physical muscle, I neglected to put the same time and effort into my continuing quest for a loving, committed relationship. I had cultivated a strong sense of self-worth. I believed in myself as a talented performer and educator. I had a genuine knowledge about sexuality. I loved being a mom and, even though Kyrsha gave me "grief" sometimes, we had an enduring bond that would smooth out the rough edges of our relationship once she grew out of her teens. I had command of my life and felt I was headed in a positive direction, even if I didn't know for sure what it would look like.

But here's the rub. I didn't have the faith and courage to do it all alone. I felt I needed a true partner. I was still *too desperate* for a relationship. As much as I had grown physically, emotionally, intellectually, and spiritually, I was not able to contend with my most terrifying fear— being alone. During the few months in between relationships, I deluded myself that I was not so desperate for male validation or companionship—that is, until the next man showed up. On the one hand, I was emotionally healthier than I had ever been. On the other, my hand constantly craved holding the hand of another. I was always reaching out, always searching for *Mr. Right*. The dilemma of needing a relationship blinded the progress I made. When I met Tony, I stopped my personal exploration just before tackling my biggest weakness and most self-sabotaging fear.

Tony was younger than I and had been living on his own since he left high school. He was a master mechanic and carpenter and ran his own small business. After our first brief encounter, we saw each other at the gym almost every day and began to learn more about each other. It soon became obvious that we wanted more time to get to know each other outside our usual weight-lifting sets.

Tony and I were mismatched from the start. Unfortunately, I could only believe in the romantic myth that duped me into thinking I was finally going to build my dream partnership. Even with all my self-esteem tools, I couldn't see that the person I had picked was unable and unwilling to create the kind of equal partnership that I needed. I forgot to take all my self-worth treasures and apply them to my choice of partner. I didn't look at Tony with the same brutal honesty to which I subjected myself.

I made allowances for him that I would never make for myself. He could be selfish and demanding, and I would accept his behavior as something he would eventually get over. He would threaten to leave the relationship, and underneath his threats, I could hear his fear, and I would accept his apology. He would call me vicious names in the heat of an argument, and I would teach him to express his anger in more positive ways. I was the understanding one who nurtured him instead of taking care of myself. I allowed his outbursts to continue, and I made excuses for them until I finally held him accountable for his attitudes and behavior. I was certainly holding myself accountable. Why should I treat him any differently than myself?

Our sex life reflected our different attitudes which, in turn, influenced our individual and relationship behaviors. What Tony thought of as "turn-ons," I thought of as sexist turnoffs. He wanted to keep everything, including our sex life, in a realm that supported his needs. Our sexual expression always started with my having to "look" sexy for him. When I tried to explain that I needed to feel sexy for me, he saw it as a sacrifice of his pleasure. He resisted participating in a partnership as strongly as I accepted my self-worth. He saw our partnership as a loss of his power instead of a gain for both of us. We weren't making an emotional connection in our lovemaking. He was fighting for control, and I was trying to create an equal partnership. My needs and feelings were DISMISSED because he thought they were going to lessen his pleasure. It was never about both of us. Tony had never learned about or felt the power of a partnership.

Once again, I closed my eyes to reality. When Tony called me horrible names, I blamed his behavior on his own shameful childhood experiences. I tried desperately to show him a better way. I thought I was being nurturing. When he screamed, "You're always helping other people instead of me," I stopped helping those I loved. When he flirted with other women at the gym, and I told him that it bothered me, he said, "It's all in your mind," and I believed him. All the while, I could hear my mother's voice: *Demand that others treat you as well as you would treat yourself.* I played the hypocrite one more time by not demanding for myself what I taught others. Tony was treating me exactly the way I treated myself, and I WASN'T TREATING MYSELF WELL. I put myself down by not believing I deserved to have a real partner who loved and respected me. I treated myself badly by believing it was my destiny to be in conflict-ridden relationships. I beat myself up with the belief that relationships would always be a struggle for me. I continued to settle for the same relationship over and over again. Same relationship, different man.

Ultimately, I had to come to terms with my fear of being alone and not having a relationship. Once and for all, I had to let go of the need to *try to get someone to love me.* I spent so much of my time constantly trying to get what I needed from a relationship, I was exhausted.

WE NEED TO IDENTIFY THE PROBLEMS IN OUR PARENTAL RELATIONSHIPS TO SUCCEED IN ANY RELATIONSHIP

ALL I HAD KNOWN from childhood was the struggle I felt to get my father to love and validate me. And I struggled with every love relationship from then on. This struggle for love was all I knew. Even though I was in a constant state of deprivation, hating it, and feeling weary, I was unable and afraid to let go of such a failing routine. This fear was my last hurdle, my *noon* wake-up call. I had to face it and finally get over it if I wanted to truly find the best love.

Tony proved to be the pinnacle of this relationship fear. We married, even though I knew he was not the right partner for me from the get go. In fact, he wasn't a partner at all. I knew it intuitively, yet I still plunged into the relationship. I knew this man. I had been with his kind many times. He had learned from his father to be the dictator. I had learned from my father to be the one dictated to, even though, on occasion, I stood my ground.

So, why did I jump into the fire again? Why did I pick another obvious bad match? Tony was just another opportunity to continue my self-imposed struggle. As much as I had learned over the course of my other relationships, Tony was a clear example of my belief that I did not deserve better.

WE HAVE TO LIBERATE OURSELVES FROM NEGATIVE CHILDHOOD MESSAGES

EVEN THOUGH I walked right into another painful relationship, one that went against all that I advocated for everyone else, I realized that this relationship mistake was part of my growth process. Fortunately, I did wake up just before the noon whistle blew. After five years of pain and struggle, I left Tony and moved to Los Angeles.

I also left behind the childhood pain of my father's rejection. I let go of the need to beat my head against a brick wall to try to get the love and respect I deserved. I left a thirty-year battle of trying to convince a lover to also be my partner. I left behind the name calling, the bullying, and all the lying, cheating, and threatening that characterized so many of my relationships—relationships that I chose. I say *chose* because I take full responsibility for my relationships and my share in their demise. I allowed my fear to rule and fuel my desperation.

So what happened that finally woke me up? I finally started to live what I was saying, walking the walk instead of just talking the talk.

- I made a conscious decision to treat myself better.

- I did not allow anyone to treat me in a lesser way than I deserved.

• I decided to hold Tony and others in my life accountable for their words and actions. If these words and actions were destructive to my self-worth, then I would remove myself from the company of those involved.

• Instead of settling for what I thought was the best I could get, I said *no* to it and selected what I truly wanted.

• If I could say *no* to certain aspects of my sex life, it was time to be consistent in every other aspect of my life.

In hindsight, it all seems so easy and simple, or as Kyrsha would say, "Duh! Mom," but I guess I had to go through a few *DUHs* before *I got it!*

SEXUALITY IS PHYSICAL, EMOTIONAL, INTELLECTUAL, AND SPIRITUAL—DON'T ACCEPT ANYTHING LESS

SEX IN A RELATIONSHIP is a good indicator of how well the rest of the partnership is going. During my marriage to Tony, I realized that there were four components of a loving relationship. When we experience sex on all four levels, we have a better chance of making our relationships pleasure filled and satisfying.

• **Physical Sex:** Some of us try to be sexual purely in a physical way, which is the way Tony enjoyed sex—for the sheer physical pleasure. Do it and be done with it. It doesn't guarantee any success for our partners. Many of us have experienced *The One-Night Stand,* only to discover that empty feeling the next morning. We may have had good physical sex to the point of orgasm, but that satisfied feeling doesn't last. Many times, during and after intercourse under these purely physical conditions, a voice inside of us keeps nagging about the lack of fulfillment, and instead of feeling good, sexual contact brings up feelings of shame. I can remember times in my life when I would have intercourse too early in the relationship. I would find myself intensely physically involved through intercourse. Yet my partner and I would have little or no spiritual connection. The relationship would teeter as if on a seesaw—overweight on the sexual side—and it was difficult, often impossible, to level out and get back into balance.

• **Emotional Sex:** Some of us focus on the emotional side of sexuality and use sex as a way to be close to someone even though we know that person isn't really in love with us. This kind of sexual experience creates more desperation than perspiration, and it is a way to set us up for hurt. This is not what sexuality is supposed to do. Sex should make us feel better about ourselves and our partners. I can remember feeling more emotionally scared and lonely *after* intercourse with Tony. My fear and insecurity was a barometer for showing me that I wasn't expressing love for myself or my partner. How could I love someone if I felt so emotionally unsafe? The physical aspects of sexuality are so much harder to enjoy when there is so much emotional insecurity.

• **Intellectual Sex:** We're playing mind games if we think of sex as a duty or obligation, something we're supposed to do. This thought process drains all passion from an intimate connection. If we feel we should do something, there is no joy in the sexual process, and we deny the physical and emotional pleasure we deserve, not only for ourselves but also our partners. Many people settle for this kind of sexual expression when they are not being honest with themselves about their own needs and desires, or they fear being vulnerable. Technically, they can perform the act well, but there is no emotional investment and, therefore, no emotional return for themselves or their partners.

• **Spiritual Sex:** Most of us rarely experience the spiritual side of sex, but this aspect of sexuality is as important, if not more important, than the other three. Our religious beliefs tend to cause us to have more guilt and shame about sex than pleasure. Our childhood experiences may have caused us to doubt ourselves and lose faith in our ability to make correct choices. My relationship with Tony was clouded by my relationship with my father. Instead of relying on my intuition, which said Tony was not the right man for me, I listened to his lies, because as with my dad, I wanted his love and approval. Spiritual sex can only be reached when we feel safe with our partners. It's having a sexual soul mate—there is no judgment or resentment between each other. It is the pinnacle of sexual satisfaction. It is sexual expression that leaves you physically relaxed, emotionally secure, intellectually stimulated, and spiritually connected. It is the best sex there is, and it *is* possible to attain. I am smiling with contentment just thinking about it. Experiencing sexuality on all four levels is what the best love is all about.

THE COMBINATION OF SEXUALITY AND SPIRITUALITY IS BETTER THAN PEANUT BUTTER AND JELLY!

I REMEMBER THE first time I tried to have sex with my husband Mark after our daughter was born. I thought to myself, *Oh my God, mothers don't act like this! They can't moan and scream during an orgasm!* It was so difficult for me to connect my new role of mother with my old role of sensuous sex partner. I had to work on adjusting my self-image. I had to see who I was as both, not as either/or. We have to see sexuality and spirituality as both, too.

The first thing I had to do, to connect what seemed like total opposites, was to bypass my religious upbringing that taught me sexuality was an enemy of my spiritual growth. I knew that if I was going to integrate my sexuality with my spirituality, I had to make them supportive partners. They had to work together as a team to help me reach a higher moral ground.

I read; I questioned; and I made a conscious effort to keep my spiritual energy in the forefront of my daily life so that it was warmed up and ready by the time I needed it to make sexual decisions. Sexual decisions were so much easier to make when I had a spiritual understanding of myself and my sexuality. My spiritual beliefs supported gender equality and total honesty and began to make sense in a practical way:

• No person was more sexually important or had more sexual rights than I.

• No one had the right to judge another purely by his or her sexual orientation.

• No person had the right to use another for his or her own sexual gratification.

• Intercourse wasn't to be used as a first-time greeting or ego boost.

Being spiritual to me means trusting in a higher awareness, which I believe is an energy far wiser than I am. It is a compassionate energy that connects and guides me through any darkness or fear. It is an honest energy, pure and unspoiled. It is not a rationalization but an intuitive intelligence. I tap into my spiritual energy when I pay attention to that quiet, gentle inner voice that tells me ways to live a more peaceful and joy-filled life.

To be spiritual in our lovemaking means there is no fear, guilt, or shame because we are using our sexuality to unite on a deeper and more meaningful level. We are not hiding a single emotion or pretending with our partners. Faking cannot survive in a spiritual atmosphere. There is no room for one-way sexual pleasure or sexual entitlement, only mutual sharing. We are in the moment, using every touch to help increase our appreciation for each other.

The most important thing to remember is that a real relationship has to have both spirituality and sexuality. Tony and I weren't on the same wavelength, and we didn't feel safe and comfortable with each other. We were spiritually disconnected because we weren't honest with each other.

When I was growing up, nothing was more comforting, pleasurable, or fulfilling than a peanut-butter-and-jelly sandwich. As the stress of my school day began to wear on me, just knowing I had this delectable sandwich waiting at lunch made it all seem better. It was a well-earned reward. It was nourishing, delicious, and so very satisfying. The other kids sitting next to me were envious—they wished for its simple yet mouthwatering taste. I could always count on my peanut-butter-and-jelly sandwich to give me pleasure, and I never got bored with its flavor.

For those who have never experienced the exquisite delight of the peanut-butter-and-jelly sandwich, try it. It's the same with the combination of sexuality and spirituality. This association is the ultimate in satisfaction, and the best combination of two of life's most powerful forces. My analogy may seem simplistic, but maybe I should have asked Tony if he liked peanut-butter-and-jelly sandwiches as much as I did.

WAKE UP! IT'S TIME FOR A SATISFYING RELATIONSHIP!

By this time, I had been talking about sexual partnerships for a few years in my *Hot, Sexy and Safer* lectures. When I finally got it, I was able to make the commitment to myself and accept only what I knew I deserved. From then on, my feelings of self-worth really took hold. I was calmer than I had ever been. I left Tony and moved to California to start a new life. In the past, I would have been crazed, but I wasn't. I wasn't afraid of being alone anymore. I wasn't bitter about another bad choice of partners. I wasn't going to beat myself for another mistake. In fact, I was proud of myself more than ever in my life.

It was noon, and I was wide awake!

CHAPTER TEN

Trusting Your Inner Wisdom to Connect with Your True Partner

Finally, I'm attracted to a man with
a sick sense of humor like mine!

RELEASING THE FEAR
SO I COULD BE MY TRUE SELF

IT SOUNDS WEIRD, but I was so happy that I had failed again. I was happy that I had made the same mistake with Tony because I knew it was my last mistake. No more self-sabotaging choices for me. I knew my marriage to Tony was a last, desperate act before I moved to a deeper and more spiritual place, one that would not tolerate my frantic energy creating a partnership with the wrong materials—the wrong person with the wrong attitude. What was I doing? A real partnership could not be built on fear: fear of being alone, fear of rejection, fear of abandonment. I could not truly build lasting self-worth until I was willing to let go of those fears.

I don't even know how to describe my feelings the day I walked out of my house leaving behind Tony, my three dogs, and all my furniture. I experienced a contentment I had never felt before. It reminded me of the Alcoholics Anonymous serenity prayer my mother taught me when I was a little girl. I kept hearing the prayer being repeated over and over in my mind, like a song one cannot help humming all day: *God grant me the serenity to accept the things I cannot change; give me the courage to change the things I can; and the wisdom to know the difference.*

• GOD GRANT ME THE SERENITY TO ACCEPT THE THINGS I CANNOT CHANGE. I couldn't change Tony or any other person except myself. He was not a good partner for me because we did not value the same things. We didn't have the same goals in our individual accomplishments or in terms of our relationship. I tried so hard to convince myself that we did. I tried to ignore our obvious conflicting differences, but I would not accept the things I could not change.

• GIVE ME THE COURAGE TO CHANGE THE THINGS I CAN. The only place I ever lacked courage was in my relationships. Otherwise, I was a huge risk taker and advocate for change. As a teenager I helped community members start a rehabilitation center for drug users. Believe me, it wasn't a service welcomed with open arms in my small-minded New England town, but we did it despite the protests. I started my own theater company with a friend and produced critically acclaimed drama and comedy. I had helped to organize one of the first dinners for people with AIDS when most of my friends were advocating quarantines for AIDS patients, or worse. Yet, in my personal, intimate relationships, I displayed little of this courage. This was my most vulnerable spot, and for many years I let fear of criticism and rejection block my better judgment. This weakness could not be healed without addressing it with the same courage I used to help change the world.

Making wrong choices in relationships because of this overwhelming fear is so obvious to me now that writing about the past seems almost unreal. I suppose that's how you can tell when you've really healed a personal wound—you can't imagine ever being in *that place again*. It's like replaying a movie in your head, only this is a movie I wrote, directed, and starred in. Today, I cannot see myself in that role. I have grown beyond it. I have a lot of the same energy and personality, but I am very different in the way I think and feel about myself. I still have certain fears about my relationship, but I can manage them. I don't feel overwhelmed and paralyzed as I used to. I am not as dependent on my partner's validation to feel good about myself, so I am much stronger emotionally. This strength comes from knowing more about myself; knowing what I need to keep my self-worth intact; and knowing how important it is to keep myself physically, emotionally, intellectually, and spiritually nourished and connected; and being honest with myself and my partner.

• GIVE ME THE WISDOM TO KNOW THE DIFFERENCE. This was certainly a problem in my relationships. I did not have a clue about which situations were changeable and which weren't. I was determined to change everything and everyone all by myself, or else. The *or else* usually meant the relationship was over and another move for Kyrsha and me.

ℒEAVING BEHIND CHILDISH ANXIETIES

THANK GOD I made that one final move to California. At age forty-three, I packed my personal possessions and started all over again. I felt like a reincarnated spirit eager to try out my new tools: self-worth and courage. This time I felt secure, not like a little kid who wants to show off new clothes while underneath harboring childlike insecurities. This time, I was truly happy to be alive and well. It was more like recovering from a long illness and being able to do all the things I hadn't been able to do. This time, I wanted to do all the things I had been afraid to do.

I was all prepared to live alone, and I looked forward to it. For the first time in my adult life, I was not looking for a partner; I felt free. Kyrsha wanted to live with me, so we agreed to look for an apartment together.

This feeling of inner peace was new to me. I had always considered myself spiritual, but this was different. Most of my life I felt like Peter Pan—not completely grown-up and always trying to get my *spiritual* shadow to stick to me permanently. But my spirituality was no longer a shadow following behind me. It became a part of myself. I learned over the years that the more I used my spiritual energy, the stronger and more connected I felt as a human being, including sexually.

OPPOSITES ATTRACT, BUT LIKES CONNECT

FOUR YEARS BEFORE I moved to Los Angeles, I met David through business associates. He was interested in producing a television special with me. I was performing my *Hot, Sexy and Safer* concert all around the country, and many friends thought it would be great for television. David was funny and charming, but I was married to Tony at the time, so I never thought about David in any other way than as a possible business partner. We saw each other periodically at meetings in Los Angeles, but nothing ever came of the television project.

Years later, when I made the decision to move to Los Angeles, David's production company called to ask me if I would be interested in developing a TV talk show with me as the host. I said yes in a flash. David and I began to meet once again, this time on a regular basis. Remember, at this time, I was not desperate to meet a man or have a relationship. I had let go of my fear of being alone. I was calm in the face of the unknown that awaited me on the West Coast. Armed with my new commitment to honesty, I embraced this new opportunity for adventure. After spending ninety-nine percent of my life in one place, I was ready and able to *accept, change, and know the difference.*

Whatever was supposed to happen, I was ready. I believed there were no coincidences in life, so meeting David was not a coincidence. He was in my life because I had finally made peace with the issue concerning my father. All my adult life I had searched for a true partner, yet I couldn't be a true partner myself with my ongoing feelings of inadequacy. I never would have known David was the right partner for me if I had not erased the fear of rejection that blocked my spiritual and emotional wisdom. As soon as I did, I was able to tap into my spiritual insight and nourish its growth.

It's easier to relate with our physical, emotional, and intellectual abilities when we are in touch with our innate inner wisdom. If psychics are able to see into the future, it's only because they are not afraid to use their spiritual sight. Many of us resist our spiritual side because we are so wrapped up in our fear and pain that we can't see the forest for the trees. We spend more time looking under the hoods of our cars or at the clothes in our closets than examining our spiritual selves.

One day, as David and I were at a meeting pitching our show idea, I saw him with my spiritual vision. Everything was so clear. I felt as if I had had a spiritual cataract operation because I was no longer looking through my fear and hurt. I often tell others that the best partner is probably standing right next to them or very close by, but we're too blinded by fear and pain to see who they are. Well, at that meeting I saw my true partner. My spiritual voice kept repeating, *There he is, silly. Congratulations! You earned this partner because you're not desperate anymore.* The inner voice was right, and I was learning to trust its accuracy more each day. Now, all I had to do was tell David.

In the past, I would have strived to make the relationship happen, but that behavior was obsolete. I did not have to control the situation. All I had to do was to honestly describe to David how I felt. If he felt the same, fine; if he didn't, I was prepared to accept the things I could not change. I could live well and be fulfilled with or without a partnership. Knowing that I was capable of living without a partner felt peculiar. I was not used to this calm inside me. My whole life had been a series of emotional inner struggles that manifested themselves in my relationships. This new inner guidance definitely made me more stable and secure. In fact, it made me more vibrant.

Thank God I still had my sense of humor because I was able to match David joke for joke, wise-ass remark for remark, and embarrass the man who was known as the "king" of embarrassment. After all, I was known as the "Sex Lady" and the "Condom Queen." I made my living using humor to inspire and educate. In me, David met his match. He just didn't know the match was for life.

Despite all the friendly bantering, I was in a predicament. I wanted to be honest and tell David how I felt about him, but he was involved in a relationship. As life would have it, the moment of truth came for David and me. I was in Los Angeles for a meeting on the TV show, and neither of us had plans for that particular Friday evening. David's girlfriend was at school, so we decided to go to a movie. As it turned out, we went to see *The Age of Innocence*, a movie about unrequited love. During the movie, I was stunned to discover that David was crying. Afterwards, we walked and talked, went for coffee, and then, David drove me home. I thanked him for an entertaining evening, and as I turned to leave, I felt compelled to be one hundred percent honest with him. Not only did I need the practice in speaking from my heart, but I felt so grateful and appreciative for what he had done for me.

I know it sounds a bit dramatic to be grateful to a man for taking me to the movies and buying me coffee, but those weren't the reasons why I wanted to thank him. I needed to thank him for just being David. Here was a man who was sensitive, aware, funny, and strong. By being attracted to a man like David, I had trusted my spiritual wisdom to make the right choices in my partnerships. I was encouraged that men like David existed and that at last I was attracted to one of them. I was finally headed in the right direction, healing old wounds that had driven me to make desperate choices.

I turned around and said, "David, I want to thank you for more than the movie and coffee. You don't know this, but I have been struggling with my fears about relationships most of my life. You have helped me so much in just the short time that I have known you. I want to let you know that I am attracted to you, but I have no intention of acting on it. That's not why I'm telling you all of this. I'm just grateful to be finally attracted to someone like you. I feel like a grown woman. I've overcome a big struggle, and I'm on the other side. I plan to find someone who has your capacity to give and nurture, and also has your sick sense of humor."

By this time I was in tears, but they were tears of relief. Finally, I felt safe enough with a man to be completely honest about my feelings. I knew I had made it. David was in shock. By this time, he had moved as far into his corner of the car as he could, his arms crossed over his chest like a protective shield across his heart.

I continued. "I'm sorry if this makes you uncomfortable, but I felt I had to let you know how grateful I was." By now I was on a roll, so I blurted out, "What confuses me, though, is why you're so unhappy. For someone who is perceptive, intelligent, and enthusiastic about life, who gives so much to others, I don't know why you believe you don't deserve the same. And I bet you're not making her very happy either. Make a decision to move on or stay together so that you both can have a love relationship you want and deserve. Don't give up. I haven't. Just know that you are worth being loved, and so is she."

His first response was, "How do you know all this?" My answer seemed pretty lame. "I don't know, I just do." Then he shared with me the stories of his past failed relationships and marriages and explained how he felt he would never really be in love or find a true partner. He was very critical of himself, and I knew how that felt. Like me, he suffered from a lack of self-worth and was ashamed of his failures. I told him, "I'm the *queen* of relationship failure. You don't have to declare yourself *king* for my sake." I had left my old court, renounced my throne, and was moving to a wiser, happier, and more peaceful existence where there were no more kings or queens, just partners.

As I left the car, he called me back and confessed that his present relationship was not working and that they had just moved back together after a six-month separation. I told him, "She deserves to know how you feel. If you're not getting what you want in the relationship, chances are she isn't either." He thanked me for my honesty. I told him, "Don't worry about me, my feelings for you have already accomplished what they were supposed to. You're my inspiration."

OUR SEXUAL LIFE HAD TO BE BUILT ON BELIEFS WE BOTH SHARED

IN THE WEEKS that followed, David and I continued to work on our TV project. Occasionally we met for coffee; otherwise, we talked long-distance on the phone. One day, he told me that he had spoken to his girlfriend about how he felt, and they had decided to separate.

David and I began to build our relationship from the spiritual to the physical, not the other way around. We didn't have intercourse for almost six months. I wanted our sex life to develop along with our emotional and spiritual life. David was a bit surprised by some of my philosophy, but he was a good sport and always willing to give it a try. When we had sex, we took our time. We made sure that with each touch, caress, or kiss, we gave each other honest feedback about how we felt and what we liked. We moved slowly, making sure we did not miss anything. We always made sure our "sick" sense of humor brought fun and pleasure into our lovemaking. Shame and embarrassment were easily diffused by attitudes that excluded judgment or criticism. Our sex life was as important as other aspects of our partnership, and it deserved attention and nurturing. It was one of our most intimate times together and the one thing we did only with each other. This was our gift to each other and to ourselves. When our schedules got hectic, we set aside a time and place to express our sexuality. And every day, we sexually teased each other as a reminder of how appreciative we were to be best friends and lovers.

David and I were married on September 30, 1995. David was such a great student and teacher. He taught me to be more verbal during our lovemaking, even while having an orgasm. I thought I was so uncoordinated that I could not talk and have an orgasm at the same time. He learned to control his need to be the aggressor. At first it was difficult because his need to control our sexual expression was a way to protect himself from being too vulnerable. So we worked on his feeling safe and loved. I gently but firmly reminded him that the best sex is the kind we design together, making sure we are both satisfied, sexually, emotionally, and spiritually. Our sexual demeanor as a couple became a reflection of our whole relationship.

I have often heard couples say, "How come we get along great in bed but don't agree on anything else?" My answer is: Anyone can master the mechanics. We are all capable of having an orgasm and good sex. Is that all we want to settle for? Most of these couples eventually break up because their sex life is not enough to keep them together. Physical sex without the emotional and spiritual components is a reflection of a one-dimensional relationship. Great sex without an emotional and spiritual partnership isn't enough to hold two people together. If you have good sex with one person without the emotional compatibility, what's to stop you from being with someone else?

We can always hide our real selves behind sex, even good sex. That means we are not willing to tackle the really important and difficult issues of a true partnership: airing our upsets, compromise, listening to one another, compassion for each other, sharing tasks, etc. What seems like great sex turns out to be only so-so compared with a sexual partnership that is emotionally, intellectually, and spiritually connected.

On the other end of this problem are couples who have a lot in common except in the bedroom. I believe these couples do not put enough time and energy into their sex life. The other areas are manageable, but when faced with a part that needs some work and time, they give up too easily. If they are dishonest in the beginning of their sex life, and don't go back and fix it, layers of resentment and fear will undermine future efforts.

We can all get caught up in the demands of everyday life or lose our passion for making our partnership the best it can be. It is too easy for most of us to live with sexual dissatisfaction. Many of us don't have many sexual tools to begin with, so trying to build a better sex life is only more frustrating. Remember the phrase "It takes two to tango"? We can't fix our sexual partnerships by ourselves. An unwilling partner can squash our enthusiasm for change in an instant. Then we think: *Why risk screwing everything up if the rest of the partnership is okay?* So we learn to live without sex. This excuse for enduring an unhappy sex life is understandable but destructive in the long run. Everyone deserves the best sexual partnership.

Write out on a piece of paper a prescription you and your partner are going to "take" to help heal your ailing sex life:

• Don't let anything or anyone—an engagement, work, or personal commitment—take precedent over fixing your sexual partnership (within reason).

• Tell each other that you both deserve a better sexual partnership and that you can only fix it together.

• Forget about the past! Look forward to new sexual excitement. Focus on what you are going to do, not what you haven't done.

ANYONE WHO WANTS TO LEARN TO BE A GREAT SEX PARTNER CAN BE ONE

THE KEY IS that you want to be a partner, and that you are willing to let go of past emotional baggage. Once you are ready to be a true partner, great sex can be achieved. Here are some steps to master that will help build a good sexual foundation:

1. IF YOU CAN'T SAY THE WORDS, DON'T DO THE DEED. Find a sex language that you and your partner feel comfortable with

and can use. There are hundreds of sex words and terms, some clinical, and some from the streets. Some sex language is sexy, and some is sexist. If a couple doesn't have the sex words to talk about their lovemaking, or can't agree on the kinds of words to use, then it will be almost impossible to agree on what they want to do sexually. Words not only have meaning, they also have an underlying connotation. How we say the words and our tone of voice play an important part in sexual communication.

Men and women are brought up with two completely opposite sex languages. Men are encouraged "to say it like it looks." *I love to see me going inside of you.* Women are taught "to say it like it feels." *It feels so good when you touch me.* Men tend to be more graphic and specific; women are more general. Many couples get stuck in language and are turned off by what their partners say. Men often complain that *she doesn't say what she wants,* and women complain that *he is too dirty in his sex talk.* Men must become aware that when they use very graphic words like *cock* or *fuck,* most women are uncomfortable. Many women are brought up to believe these are dirty words used mostly in porn films or in anger. Women must learn that men are not mind readers and that graphic sex words between lovers aren't dirty if they are spoken with love.

If we value a great sexual relationship, then we must design a language that expresses both love and sexual pleasure. A combination of both styles makes for better sexual communication. Choose words that are explicit *and* express caring, but don't use any sexist words because these are put-downs, not turn-ons. Negotiate and compromise. For instance, the other evening David called to tell me "I loved our sex last night." It meant so much to hear him say that because we had been arguing the night before about the mess he had left in our office. "I can't work here when it's so disorganized," I had told him. He instantly got defensive and said, "It figures you'd start an argument just before bed and ruin the mood for making love." I replied, "I'm not angry about anything you do in the bedroom. This is about keeping the office more organized. The minute I walk out of this office, my anger stays here, and I'm very ready to make love in the bedroom. I hope you can do the same." He smiled and said, "I can if you can. And, I'll do better in the office, hopefully as well as I do in the bedroom."

That moment for David and me illustrates how important our sexual expression is to the well-being of our relationship. We don't take our sexual activity for granted. He called to tell me how much he enjoyed what WE did, not what I did *to* him or *for* him. We didn't let a completely separate issue get in the way of our lovemaking. Without clear communication and direction, most of us would never get to half the places we want to go.

2. OPEN YOUR EYES AND LET IN SOME LIGHT. I can't believe how many times I've said

to David or Kyrsha when they are looking for something in the fridge, "Open your eyes, and you'll find it!" Or if I'm helping a friend to admit that she has a problem, I'll say, "Open your eyes. Can't you see what this person is doing to you?" I feel the same about sex. Keeping our eyes closed or being in the dark during sexual interplay perpetuates embarrassment and shame. Most of us close our eyes when we are afraid to see something like a scary movie or even a real-life tragedy. But if we aren't ready to watch ourselves do a sexual act, we aren't ready to do that act. We must see what we are really doing sexually so that we can understand why we are doing it. Furthermore, we will gain more pride in our sexuality when we are able to watch ourselves and celebrate the beauty of sex. Believe me, it is much better to watch ourselves making love than two actors pretending to have sex in a movie.

Another important thing is not to use the darkness to hide what you believe is an unattractive body. It's time for all of us to reject the artificial standard of sexiness and beauty forced on us by the media and advertisers. Women are the worst offenders. We need to actively reject these "body perfect" images that are thrown at us all day long. We all look sexy when we are sexually happy and satisfied and when we are confident of our giving and receiving of sexual pleasure.

3. WE MUST PLEASURE OURSELVES WITHOUT PRESSURE TO REACH OR-

GASM. We are too result oriented, trying to reach orgasm, instead of enjoying the process of pleasure. A rushed and pressure-filled process can actually inhibit our pleasure and sabotage the result. The Best Love Theory is: Learning to give and receive pleasure is one of the most important goals in creating sexual confidence and satisfaction. Reaching orgasm is easier when it is the result of building pleasure and sexual excitement. Learn to experience *climbing to climax.* Don't jump off the cliff with your eyes closed. Accepting pleasure is the basis for sexual satisfaction and reaching orgasm. Always check to see if you are rushing or skipping steps in the sexual pleasure process. If you are bored or tired with your sexual routine, you have stopped exploring pleasure avenues. You have become result-oriented instead of passionate and nurturing. If you are having trouble reaching orgasm, you may be stressed by trying to reach the goal without filling your body and soul with sexual pleasure. The Best Sex is about the process. Take your time and connect with your partner.

4. WE CAN HAVE ORGASMS WITHOUT PENIS PENETRATION. Once you begin the process of pleasure, and you feel more comfortable, encourage (don't demand or push) the giving and receiving of more pleasure without any penetration of the penis. This is how we really start to redefine sex and sexual satisfaction. It is also the start of learning how to make intercourse mutually satisfying. When you have discovered at least one

way to bring yourself and your partner to orgasm
with just touching and rubbing, try other ways. For
instance, use other parts of your body, like a strong
thigh, the breasts, an arm, or a back, and other positions to gain greater contact with the clitoris and
the penis, but don't push for the result. Everyone
is different, and some ways to reach orgasm will
be easier, and some will need more time and coax-
ing. Discovering new ways to have orgasms without intercourse should be part of your sexual
growth process for the rest of your life. Remember to use your hands. Our hands are our best love
makers. For women, use your fingers and his fingers to explore outside and inside your vulva and
vagina. Move from the clitoris to the opening of
the vagina and then to the upper wall of the vagina.
There are four hands between the two you, so use
them all and take turns. Never think you cannot
reach orgasm a certain way. Instead say to yourself, *I'm exploring this sexual behavior and learning to
increase my pleasure.*

If you have a real aversion to certain sexual
foreplay or stimulation, tell your partner openly
and honestly and take some time to examine why.
Many of our aversions are learned through bad experiences or being shamed when we were young.
Of course, there are limits to sexual pleasures, and
we certainly should not have to do anything that
is painful or humiliating. No one's sexual pleasure
should be dependent on doing something that
could truly hurt. Each of us has the right to decide
what we want to learn or do and how we want

to expand our sexual pleasure. Take these steps slowly, and don't let your partner control the process. If you work together, you will reach greater mutual satisfaction and have more fun, too.

I remember the first time I started touching myself during foreplay with David. I remember the look on his face as he watched my hands move back and forth from me to him to me again. First, he watched in amazement, and then he smiled. I asked him if he was uncomfortable by my pleasing myself. He was not, and in fact, it was a turn-on. It also helped to take the pressure off him to be my ultimate satisfier. It gave him an opportunity to learn about me and what I liked.

5. SHOW AND TELL WHAT YOU HAVE LEARNED. This is one of my favorite steps because it is the beginning of building a true partnership that celebrates mutual satisfaction. Now that you have touched, rubbed, and kissed your way to an orgasm, it's time to show and tell your partner what you have learned and what more you want to explore together. Every man and woman should feel and watch his or her partner have an orgasm. Men, while your partner is rubbing her clitoris, you can feel your partner's orgasm by sliding one or two fingers into her vagina. When she reaches orgasm, you will feel the vagina tighten and go into contractions. Her PC muscle, which is around the opening of the vagina, is strong and has a good grip so you can feel these contractions easily. Women, you should feel and

see your partner's penis push out his orgasm while
he masturbates.

You may wonder why I think it's important
to watch your partner have an orgasm. I am proud
of my orgasms. I am not ashamed or embarrassed
to show them to David. I'm not embarrassed by
the faces I make, or the noises I make, or the funny
way my body twists like a pretzel. This is the real
me. My orgasm is one of my most vulnerable moments, and sharing it with David brings us even
closer. I admire his moments of pleasure just as
much as I enjoy mine because I understand that he
is accepting his sexuality as an important part of
who he is. An orgasm is just one more expression
of self-worth and self-esteem, and when both partners feel pleasure from their orgasms, the relationship can only get better.

The purpose of being able to watch and talk
about your sexual pleasure is to make sure that mutual satisfaction is given the same opportunity for
success as anything else. Why should successful sex
be any different from successful business, recreation, or parenting? *Show and tell* time lets your
partner know, see, and feel the truth about your
process of satisfaction. Think of it as giving your
partner a gift of information that will help him or
her to be your best lover.

Does this all sound a little bit out of the ordinary to
you? Actually, what we are working on is a commonsense
approach to building sexual self-confidence and honesty

between partners. The best love and the best sex don't depend on magic tools or exotic rules; they need a commonsense step-by-step process based on positive attitudes, correct information, and a willingness to be honest with yourself and your partner.

CHAPTER ELEVEN

The New Sexual Evolution: Changing Our Attitudes About Sex and Relationships

We can have the best love and the best sex right here on earth!

SEXUAL TECHNIQUE IS NOT MUCH HELP WITHOUT SEXUAL SELF-ESTEEM

I purposely didn't put a lot of sexual technique and "how to's" in this book. I have read most sex books on the market, and even though I might have learned how to give better oral sex from a book, I never learned how to love myself more as a sexual being. Most of what I read didn't help me to change my negative sexual attitudes and fears. Often, trying new sexual positions or actions without sexual confidence only set me up to feel more guilty and ashamed of myself.

What I really needed from those sex books was someone who could teach me about all the conflicting sexual messages that were swirling around in my head. I needed some good old-fashioned inspiration to let me know that I wasn't a sexual weirdo or loser. Millions of people, just like me, are lost in a sexual maze. We seem to go down the same path over and over again and never quite get off it and on to a new one. Too many of us live double lives by hiding our unspoken desires and sexual preferences. Childhood abuse is reaching epidemic proportions. It continues to wreak havoc on so many lives by leaving deep wounds on our souls that often take a lifetime to heal, if they heal at all.

I'm all for improving our sexual technique so that our sexual interaction gives mutual pleasure and satisfaction, but only after we have changed our sexual attitudes. Just knowing *how to* without *why* and *wherefore* is definitely not enough.

My attitudes were like underpowered engines trying to move my body and soul in a direction that led me right back to where I always started from: hurt, humiliation, fear, and failure. I wasn't a bad person, yet I did some bad things. I wasn't a dishonest person, yet I did dishonest things. I wasn't a stupid person, yet I did some very stupid things. I was a major contradiction, and the more I tried to change, the more I did not. Finally, I went to the source of my behavior problems: my attitudes. I ripped them apart, strand by strand, testing each fiber to see where it came from, how strong it was, and how it powered my behavior. My attitudes came from belittling messages about being a girl, then a woman, my father's rejection and criticism, and some degrading and stupid behavioral choices.

I was a self-esteem mess. It took me the past twenty years
to discover new sexual attitudes as I scouted out my physical, emotional, and spiritual landscape, trying new paths
and new ideas. It's not hopeless or even so difficult. If I
can do it, so can you. I was just as lost, scared, and ignorant as everyone else.

FIRST, TAKE A CLOSE AND HONEST LOOK AT YOUR SEXUAL HISTORY

I WAS SEXUALLY molested as a child. A close family
friend and "father figure" attacked me on a boat when I
was ten. He put his fingers in my vagina but passed out
before he penetrated me with his penis. I cheated on a husband, and have had one-night stands. I engaged in intercourse while under the influence of alcohol and pot. I
made love with another woman. I have had more sexual
experiences than some and fewer than others.

Comparatively, my sex life has been pretty average. I
think I like variety and kinkiness as much as the next person. Where my sex life is very different, and maybe even
extraordinary, is how connected it now is on all levels—
physically, emotionally, and spiritually.

Today, my sex life has no shame, guilt, or embarrassment. I have no shame because I don't do anything of
which I am ashamed or that goes against my commitment
to being honest. As for anything hurtful that I have done
in my past, I have made apologies to myself and others
whom I've hurt. In return, I have received forgiveness
from them and have forgiven myself. I have no guilt be-

cause I take full responsibility for my actions and have admitted my mistakes to myself and others. I am not embarrassed about any aspect of my sex life because I have accepted sexuality as a normal and integral part of my well-being. I am proud of my sexuality, and take charge of it so that I can get to better physical, emotional, and spiritual places. Embarrassment comes when we try to present an untruthful image of ourselves to our partners. I am who I appear to be—the good and the not so good. I'm working on the not-so-good part, and I'm not even embarrassed about these obvious flaws because I have overcome my fears of rejection and criticism and I feel better about who I have become. Don't think for a moment that I've reached some pinnacle of sexual perfection. I'm still working on my individual sexual well-being and my partnership with David.

Second, WE NEED TO BECOME MATURE IN OUR ATTITUDES ABOUT SEX

OUR SEXUALITY IS an opportunity to expand the quality of our lives. It is sad for me to think about how, as a society, we have made sexual expression into everything it's not supposed to be. We have made the expression of love into a weapon, using sex to assault, abuse, and degrade. We have taken a beautiful and effective means of communication and made it into something dirty and shameful by using it as barter for money and status. We make it impossible to talk about sex among lovers and family members for fear we may reveal too much about our own sexual ignorances and indiscretions. We have allowed a deeply spiritual connection to be used as a superficial ego boost. As pop culture has reduced the intrinsic value and importance of sexual expression to magazine centerfolds and stag movies, most religions have added unnecessary guilt and shame to a pleasurable and natural experience. These two contradictory interpretations of the true meaning of sexual expression have left generation after generation sexually lost and confused.

It's ironic that we have to get a marriage license, a driver's license, and a license to do a myriad of jobs, but when it comes to sexual relationships, we prefer to stay uninformed. We should require a sex license to ensure that everyone has correct sexual information. This license would be subject to Sexual Safety Laws. According to the Sexual Safety Laws, it would be illegal to:

1. Have sex while under the influence of drugs and alcohol.
2. Have sex too soon in a relationship. There must be a period during which you first connect on an emotional and spiritual level.
3. Not wear a condom or use birth control while having sex.
4. Have sex that will endanger anyone.
5. Have sex in the dark. Turn on some lights.
6. Take a turn during sex without signaling your partner.
7. Lie to your partner while having sex.

8. Use sex for illegal or illicit purposes.

9. Force someone to have sex with you when he
   or she doesn't want to.

Of course, if we didn't uphold these laws, there would
be penalties. The point, is we are so desperate for the
pleasure and power of sex but not mature enough to make
it a positive force in our lives. How mature are we if we
giggle when someone says the word *penis* or *vagina?* We
can enjoy the sex life we deserve if we change our attitudes and grow up sexually, by making some promises to
ourselves and our relationships.

**HERE ARE MY TEN BEST LOVE,
BEST SEX PROMISES:**

I promise to:

1. Acknowledge my right to have a mutually satisfying sex life.

2. Take responsibility for my own sexual satisfaction.

3. Learn more about who I am as a sexual person
and work toward greater sexual self-esteem.

4. Use my sexuality for physical, emotional, intellectual, and spiritual fulfillment and pleasure.

5. Keep my sexuality as an important part of my
life and relationship.

6. Be honest with myself and my partner about where I am sexually, and where I want to be in the future, so we can grow together and not apart.

7. Never use my sexual love as a weapon, threat, ego boost, or punishment.

8. Never allow anyone to use me as a sexual object.

9. Let go of unwarranted shame, guilt, and fear that stops me from becoming sexually proud and confident.

10. Help our children and the following generations avoid the myths, misconceptions, mistakes, and unnecessary pain and hurt that accompany a sex life that does not value each partner's intrinsic worth and humanity.

THIRD, WE HAVE TO DEBUNK THE MYTHS AND MISCONCEPTIONS ABOUT SEX

SO WHAT ARE these myths and mistakes that cause pain and hurt? We want to help ourselves and our children avoid them. Let me ease everyone's worst fears, and clear up the sexual misconceptions that have contributed to our sexual ignorance. I have been talking about these ideas throughout the book, but they are worth repeating. We need a new understanding of sex, one that will contribute to everyone's sexual self-esteem.

MYTH #1. **Women Need Love More Than Sex.** False!!! Everyone needs love more than sex. When we are in a love relationship, we all need sexual intimacy and satisfaction, and we all need to be touched and validated sexually. It is the one intimate expression that sets our relationships apart from all others. With few exceptions, a love relationship without sex is empty and damaging to both individuals. Sex without love is also empty compared with sex bathed in love and appreciation.

MYTH #2. **Men Need Sexual Release More Than Women.** No man who has ever witnessed a woman's orgasm would dare say or think this. How can a man's orgasm be more important than a woman's orgasm? I'm sure a man's erection has something to do with this misconception. I admit that its hardness and ability to defy gravity is impressive, but this outer manifestation doesn't mean the inner release is more powerful. Yes, testosterone is one element of sexual drive, but research has also proven that too much testosterone can lessen and even stop this powerful desire. Ask any professional bodybuilder who has overdosed on testosterone. The body may get extra big and hard, but the penis and testicles don't enlarge, and the sex drive doesn't increase. A woman's body chemistry contains some testosterone, but hormones do not exclusively create sexual desire and need for satisfaction.

MYTH #3. **Men Are More Visual, and Women Are More Touching.** What this means is that men need and want to *watch* more during sex. How do we know if this desire to keep their eyes open is genetic or learned? After all, since adolescence men are constantly bombarded with countless pictures and images of naked women. We give men permission and encouragement to watch sex. We add to this misconception by saying women don't like to watch anything sexual because they are less visual and more into touch. I don't believe that touching is necessarily a female "trait." Women's affinity to touch may be more historical than natural. We are taught to be passive in our lovemaking. How silly and inaccurate it is to constantly put the genders at opposite poles when we are trying to build partnerships. Women have eyes for watching, and men have hands and nerve endings for experiencing touch. We need to let individuals decide their sexual responses for themselves, and not insist that touching and watching are specific gender traits. It is important for both partners to open their eyes to see what they are doing sexually as well as share in the giving and receiving of physical touch.

MYTH #4. **Men Masturbate More Than Women.** This is a half-truth. Yes, today more men do masturbate, but the numbers are changing. More women are feeling better about who they are sexually and want to know how they work and how to please themselves. It's all about permission, not gender. Maybe there will be more gender equality in other aspects of our lives when we all feel better about sexually satisfying ourselves. My new slogan is: *Reach Out and Touch Yourself.*

MYTH #5. **Women Take Longer to Reach Orgasm.** This is another half-truth. Most men, but not all, can reach an orgasm quicker than their female partners. Remember the idea about permission? When it comes to orgasms, men have had more practice and more encouragement. Many women have shared with me their concerns about how long it takes them to have an orgasm. Their concerns are partly due to the quickness of their male partners. But it's also a million times easier to achieve something when we are told and shown how. We all know how men have orgasms. Women need information about how their bodies work and encouragement so that they can be more comfortable with the length of time it takes them to reach orgasm. The fact remains, quicker is not better. The best sex is all about enjoying the process.

MYTH #6. **An Erection Is Proof That a Man Is Sexually Aroused. A Soft Penis Means He Is Not Turned On**. An erection is a sign that the nerve endings in the penis have signaled the valves to close, thus trapping blood in the tissue. Just because a man has an erection doesn't mean he is ready to have an orgasm or can have an orgasm. It's a reflex—one that can happen many times during the night and when he wakes up to pee. Conversely, if a man has a soft penis, it doesn't mean he isn't sexually aroused or enjoying the sexual experience. We place far too much emphasis on the size and hardness of a man's penis, neglecting the sensuality of his mind and the love in his heart. I have been guilty of thinking that my partner wasn't aroused because he didn't get an instant erection or because his penis didn't stay hard during all of our foreplay. I was more concerned about how much this man desired me than how we were caring for each other as friends and lovers. An erect penis is necessary for vaginal intercourse, but a man's hands will always be his most important sexual tool.

MYTH #7. **All Women Are Multiorgasmic.** If men have suffered from erection pressure, women are now subject to multiorgasm pressure. I find this so amazing since we still don't talk honestly or openly about how women have *one* real orgasm. Sexuality is not about quantity. Sexual satisfaction should always be about quality. It doesn't matter whether a woman or a man has one orgasm or five; it matters how they feel about their sexuality and sexual partnership. Trying to make a woman have six orgasms might be more an ego boost for the

man who is trying to do the satisfying. It is another
way of using sexual pleasure for the wrong reasons.
There are times when I can have more than one
orgasm, but believe me, one great orgasm is more
than enough pleasure for me. Don't place importance on the number of orgasms; instead, place
value in the feelings of contentment and satisfaction. The multiorgasm rule is: *Everyone should be in
charge of his or her orgasm(s), how they want to have
them, and how many.*

MYTH #8. **Men Reach Their Sexual Peak in
Their Teens and Early Twenties. Women
Reach Their Sexual Peak in Their Late Thir-
ties and Forties.** Here we go again. We perpet-
uate another myth about gender difference by
attributing sexual differences to biology and hormones instead of socialization. How could any
woman reach a sexual high point in her teens or
twenties when she is brought up to deny her sexual desires? To have strong sexual urges as a girl is
to risk being labeled "nymphomaniac" or "slut."
It's that *permission* thing again. Women tend to
feel more comfortable with their sexuality later in
life because it takes that long to get over all that
shame and fear. Over time, as we become more
confident in a general sense, we become more
comfortable about seeking sexual satisfaction. That
comfort level happens when we become more
knowledgeable about our bodies and our sexual
feelings. As a teen, I remember thinking about sex
and feeling sexual all day long. Every innocent re-

mark could be taken to mean something sexual. The difference between the boys and girls was that boys openly acknowledged their interest in and desire for sex. They were expected to act on their yearning. I remember watching the movie *Grease*. It was a great example of how young men and women are expected to deal with their sexual urges. When the boys bragged about scoring, they were elevated to great status. When the female characters did the same, they were labeled sluts. Maybe when sexual behavior expectations are more similar for men and women, our sexual desire or drive will be closer in age and intensity.

MYTH #9. **Women's Orgasms Come from Stimulating the G-Spot, Which Is Located in the Vagina.** Here is one of the biggest misconceptions that has plagued women for years. The G-spot is not some magical little spot that needs special attention like something you would point out to your dry cleaner. In fact, all women do not experience the same kind of sensation inside their vaginas. The real problem with the G-spot theory is that it creates another misconception about where women receive their sexual pleasure. This G-spot theory only seems to justify that a woman should get her pleasure by having a man put his penis in her vagina. This is not valid. But, isn't the penis made to fit perfectly and hit the right spot? No one knows for sure. So how could Dr. Grafenberg tell us to search (sometimes for years) for a tiny spot on the inside of our vaginas called the

"G-spot" (named after him, of course)? Even Freud added to the confusion by professing that women had two kinds of orgasms—the immature ones and the mature ones? *Huh?* The G-spot supposedly supports Freud's theory that the only mature orgasm for women is in the vagina. We shouldn't ignore all of Dr. Freud's work, but it seems we should rethink some of his theories now that several biographers state that he was addicted to cocaine, which probably contributed to his well-documented battle with sexual impotence. The glitch in Dr. G's theory is that some women have this spot, and some don't. Here's the truth. A woman's orgasm is not waiting inside a vagina for a penis to push its way in and release it. Our orgasmic nerve endings are and always will be in our clitoris. Every woman is born with a clitoris and can achieve an orgasm through direct stimulation. This is how we were meant to work. The function of the clitoris has one purpose: to create orgasms for the woman. The G-spot is merely an extension of the nerve endings in the clitoris. In other words, all women have what it takes to be orgasmic.

MYTH #10. **Vaginal Intercourse Is the Most Satisfying Sexual Act and Is the Only Real Sex**. This is the most destructive, misinformed statement that is still being passed along to generations of women. It is preposterous that young women are told that intercourse is supposed to be the most satisfying act and men are encouraged, if not obligated, to impose intercourse on women. Most women do not have an orgasm through intercourse alone. Vaginal intercourse is good for creating children, and after all, none of us would . be here without it. However, this one sexual act is not the ultimate satisfier for women, and it's time someone said so. Let's start clearing up these misconceptions so that we can get on with becoming sexually proud and confident.

FINALLY, WE NEED TO CHANGE OUR PERSPECTIVES ON INTERCOURSE

THROUGH INTERCOURSE, we can experience a special kind of closeness. Intercourse has the potential to reveal our vulnerability. It can comfort us while thrilling us, and bring out our deepest passion and pleasure. On the other hand, it can also make us feel used, abused, unloved, worthless, afraid, embarrassed, ashamed, angry, and resentful. Something so powerful should be explained in explicit terms with an emphasis on its value and place in the step-by-step process of sexual maturity. Intercourse should not be the first major sexual experience we have with a partner, rather it is a goal we should work up to over a period of time after experiencing other kinds of sexual expression.

Intercourse is not:

- **AN OBLIGATION.** Having intercourse is not a right, even when we are married. It is a sexual act that needs to be mutually agreed upon and not used as a threat, or by force. It is an expression of love and mutual consideration.

• A MEANS TO FIX ALL THE ILLS OF A RE-LATIONSHIP. Intercourse cannot be the only glue used to keep a fractured relationship together. In fact, it can sometimes make matters worse, by putting pressure on an already strained couple.

• A MALE ENTITLEMENT. Sexual intercourse should be viewed as an equal opportunity for satisfaction, assertiveness, sharing power, giving and receiving of pleasure, and feeling good about ourselves and our relationship.

The key perspective we need to change is the notion that men are in charge of the intercourse experience, that a man "does it" to a woman. Clearly, men are part of the decision-making process of when and how a couple will have intercourse. But, the woman has the final say. It is her body, and she will decide when someone else will enter it.

This change in attitude puts men and women on equal ground and always makes intercourse an affirmation of equality. It also maintains that a woman has the right to decide when the penis goes in, how far, what it can do, how long it stays, and when it comes out. In a truly loving relationship in which each partner's pleasure is equally important, this new attitude won't be a problem. In fact, it will be helpful. Let's explore how.

Most men complain that their partners are not assertive enough, especially during intercourse. *I wish she was more into it,* or *I wish she took the initiative.* With this new attitude of respect for a woman's right to be in control of her own body, a woman will want to participate more in the intercourse experience because her pleasure is increased. As she enjoys it more, her partner's pleasure will increase.

So how does this new attitude of equality change intercourse behavior? In several ways, all of which guarantee mutual satisfaction.

Intercourse should always start when the woman says she is ready and wants to be penetrated. And, trust me, the vagina will exhibit very clear signs of its readiness. When the clitoris is stimulated, the woman begins to feel sexually excited. As the sensation moves through her nerve endings, the opening of the vagina starts to expand and secretes lubrication. As the woman gets closer to orgasm, the vagina gets wider, longer, and more receptive. Just before orgasm, the vagina fills up with blood and then starts to close in until it senses a penis.

Before we go further into the intercourse experience, this biological fact about the vagina's ability to widen and then close should lay to rest any fear that a man's penis could be too small for his partner's vagina. All vaginas have the ability to take up the slack! This adjusting to genital size only happens when both partners are sexually aroused. When a woman truly feels sexually excited, her clitoris and vagina will demonstrate it.

The major problem with achieving this mutual arousal is intercourse technique. We make it look as though women have orgasms from only vaginal penetration, not clitoral stimulation. The fact is that ninety-nine percent of all intercourse positions pictured in books never show the clitoris. For a woman to reach orgasm during a variety of intercourse positions, her clitoris must be stimulated by herself or her partner. Our hands play an important role before and during intercourse. Every position of intercourse can be adjusted so that the woman's or man's hand can reach and touch her clitoris. It is not difficult to learn if we change our idea of what intercourse is supposed to be.

We have already discovered that the clitoris is the "orgasm center" for women and that the vaginal opening has a continuation of these nerve endings in the first two inches of the upper wall. When this vaginal wall area is also touched and rubbed, it helps most women to come to orgasm. For most men, the greatest area of sensation is the first two inches of their penis, so it makes sense that both these two-inch areas come into contact.

For this to happen during intercourse, I recommend that the man insert the first two inches of his penis in his partner's vagina and position himself or have his partner position herself in a way that pushes the penis up against the upper wall. The opening of the vagina (the PC muscle) and the first two inches are the tightest parts of the vagina, so both partners will feel more sensation. The best positions are: (1) when the woman is on her knees and leaning on her shoulders, leaving her hands free to touch her clitoris; or (2) when both partners are on their sides facing each other with their upper bodies about a foot and a half apart. These are just two positions that I have discovered that work for the "two-inch theory." Enjoy discovering your own variations, and let me know how they work. Thank goodness we can get past the *I have too small a penis* fear. Two inches works just fine.

This new definition of intercourse, which includes manual clitoral stimulation, also encourages partners to look at each other, talk, and even smile and laugh during the experience. It ensures mutual satisfaction and can even encourage simultaneous orgasms because both partners are actively helping the sexual experience. You will be able to tell your partner when you are about to reach orgasm and watch the ecstasy on your partner's face. Your foreplay will be more enjoyable because you know it is leading you to a pleasure-filled process and an intense result. In other words, the pressure is off, and no one partner has to *do it* to the other.

I struggled for years with unsatisfying intercourse experiences, thinking that there was something wrong with me. The only way I could have an orgasm through intercourse was when I was on top, but it took much work and effort. However, when I masturbated, I had an orgasm more easily, and it took less time. So, it wasn't me! It was the old concept of intercourse geared to the man's pleasure and satisfaction. I learned to adjust what I thought intercourse was supposed to be or look like. When I see pictures of couples having intercourse without manual clitoral stimulation, it looks strange to me.

All these new ideas take practice, but most of all, they take a patient and loving commitment that validates the similarities between men and women and our compatibility as great sex partners.

A WORD TO PARENTS: HAVING A SEX LIFE WHEN CHILDREN ARE AROUND TAKES SOME PLANNING

RECENTLY, my daughter moved into her own apartment. It's only a few blocks down the street, but it's still a move away from home. I will miss her, but I will also enjoy the privacy. David and I haven't had many moments when we could run around our home naked and playful. I'm sure that's why couples with kids enjoy going to hotels. Being away from the kids allows couples to get in touch with their sexual selves. It's difficult to move between our parent and lover roles while trying to meet all the needs of those we love. It takes effort and energy to balance the scales between doing for others and doing for ourselves.

If you want to achieve some semblance of sanity and sexual fulfillment, give yourself permission to be both a parent and a sexual being. After all, it was sex that made you a parent, so the two parts must be able to coexist! As your children get older, remember that kids do what we do, not what we say. If you're a single parent and you don't want your teenager to have intercourse, there is more of a chance that he or she will wait if you don't have intercourse early in your relationships. Kids see the world from an either/or perspective. The intricate issues of relationships and sex can be too complicated for a young person to grasp fully.

I am still guiding my twenty-three-year-old daughter through difficult decisions and scary choices. Kyrsha and

I talk a lot about sex and have many in-depth discussions about our own personal experiences. She is trying to figure out herself as a woman and how to create an equal relationship with a man. She struggles as I did with self-confidence and fear. She is confused by the mixed messages she receives in a world that still refuses to allow women to share power and control with men. Sometimes she's furious about the obvious unfair standards that govern male and female roles. Other times she seeks the praise we bestow on women who fit the ideal, but false, female image. To say the least, it's confusing for her and her male friends.

SEXUAL SATISFACTION HELPS TO KEEP US HEALTHIER

AS A RESULT of our new attitudes and behavior, we will soon discover that sexual satisfaction can help keep us healthier. Orgasms can cure allergies. They are a natural decongestant and can help to reduce migraine headaches, by increasing blood flow and reducing pressure. Orgasms also produce endorphins, which add to our feeling of well-being and stimulate our immune systems. Orgasms help lower the chances of prostate cancer in men, and for women, they keep our genitals lubricated and stronger. Lack of use causes our genitals to dry up and lose elasticity. It's the *use it or lose it* idea which relates to the second part of this theory: Sexuality needs to be used to stay alive. If our body muscles aren't used, they won't demand to be used, and when called upon to perform, they may resist and even give up. Our sexual desire also lessens with lack of use. Think of the mechanics of your car—it runs smoother and better with steady use. The same goes for the simple act of walking—the more you do it, the more you can do it. Great sex encourages more great sex, and it gives us a feeling of closeness, belonging, and being cared for like no other experience.

Over forty percent of all sexual problems are caused by health problems. As a society, we are so oblivious of the obvious connection between physical fitness and sexual fitness. I have always been an athlete, dancer and weight trainer. I have seen the changes in my body, but more importantly, I have felt the changes in my attitude about life and my sexuality. I want to nurture my sexuality and be in control of its direction and quality. I can only have the kind of sex life I want when I am physically, emotionally, and spiritually fit.

I have met so many people who try all kinds of exotic elixirs to improve their sex life and increase their sexual desire. But they often neglect the obvious: keeping themselves in better shape. If we're making a commitment to better sex, then we have to make the same commitment to better health and fitness. Maintain sexual fitness through good nutrition and an exercise plan that increases strength, flexibility, and stamina. Going to the gym definitely helped to improve my self-esteem while keeping me in shape. Now, whenever I see an ad for a fitness club or program, I want to contribute: AND YOUR SEX LIFE WILL IMPROVE GREATLY, TOO!

THERE IS SO MUCH TO LEARN, CHANGE, AND REARRANGE ALONG LIFE'S WAY

MY FAILURE TO make the best sexual choices came from not knowing what I wanted or needed to value. We hear so much talk about family values, yet most of us haven't made a commitment to our own individual values—the ideas and beliefs that guide our life decisions. I had to sit down and seriously think about what was important to me. Once I made a tangible list, I then worked to live within its guideposts. I made a commitment to myself and what I believed in.

Here is a value system, a few guideposts that can help point the way to becoming sexually proud and confident:

1. We must value ourselves and our gender. There can be no physical, emotional, or spiritual bashing of any gender or sexual orientation. When we judge another or put someone down to make ourselves feel better, we lessen our own value.

2. Being satisfied with your sex life is the same as being satisfied with who you are. You cannot build a sex life on a foundation of insecurity. Your sex life will thrive when you begin to cultivate an attitude of confidence.

3. To remain sexually ignorant is to be afraid of the power of knowledge. It's inconceivable that

our society promotes sexual ignorance. I don't trust anyone who advocates keeping sex a secret.

4. Hating your body is hating the home of your spirit. My spiritual energy radiates through my body, and I can't express love and sensual pleasure through a body I hate.

5. Passing sexual wisdom on to our children is a responsibility that we must never ignore. If we want to enjoy the gifts of sexual gratification, we can continue to partake in our sex life only if we promise to guide others.

A few parting words of wisdom: Take your sexual life seriously but never lose your sexual sense of humor. Some of the best laughs I have ever had occurred while engaging in a sexual activity, sometimes with just myself! Humor is our safety valve. It relieves the pressure built up from our fear of rejection, and shame. It lessens our resentment and calms our stress-filled hearts and minds. Laughing about or over a sexual moment is not the same as laughing at someone. Participate in the humor, and you will receive the reward of laughter.

If you are confused and afraid of your sexuality, then spend more time talking about your sexual life than you devote to talking about your job, family, friends, or hobbies. People thought I was nuts because I talked so openly about who I was as a sexual person, and what I was doing. But that openness gave me the strength and courage to examine and discover the positive and negative aspects of my sexuality. How else could I overcome so many myths and